Precipice:

The Literary Anthology
of
Write on Edge

Precipice
Volume I

ISBN: 061570462X
ISBN-13: 978-0615704623

Write on Edge

PRECIPICE COMMITTEE

Editor-in-Chief	Cameron D. Garriepy
Assistant Editor	Angela Amman
Readers	Angela Amman
	John Batzer
	Nancy Campbell
	Mandy Dawson
	Cheryl Rosenberg

STAFF

Founding Editor	Cheryl Rosenberg
Managing Editors	Angela Amman
	Cameron D. Garriepy
Assistant Editor	Mandy Dawson
Technical Advisor	John Batzer

ACKNOWLEDGEMENTS

The Editorial Committee would like to thank everyone whose contributions to both The Red Dress Club and Write on Edge have made this community such a vibrant one.

We are nothing without you.

For their part in creating the community, our heartfelt thanks to former editors Ericka Clay, Nichole Beaudry, Kate Sluiter, Galit Breen, and Nancy Campbell.

CONTENTS

Non-Fiction

Fiction

Draw your chair up close to the edge of the precipice and I'll tell you a story.

~F. Scott Fitzgerald

Non-fiction

STARSTRUCK
ANGIE KINGHORN

Everything was fried, the candy bars, the pickles, the very air around the vendors, but we chose the funnel cake. Two paper plates beneath it made a halfhearted attempt to contain the grease. My father held a wad of napkins under the plates and we tore off pieces of fried dough dusted with powdered sugar, watching the diverse and somehow homogenous stream of humanity pour down the midway.

"My gawd," he said. "Look at that!"

My 11-year-old eyes looked through the crowd, searching for "that."

"What, the guy with all the tattoos?"

"No, the woman behind him — there, see, with her thong hanging out the top of her jeans!"

"Wow."

We munched and watched until about half of the

funnel cake remained, maintaining a running narrative about the mullets, farmers' tans, and Hypercolor shirts that meandered by.

"What next?" Dad asked.

"I still want to do that singing thing," I said.

"No, you don't."

"Yes, I do! Please! Please let me!"

"You really want to?"

"Yes! Buffy and I did it together last year. We sang 'Papa Don't Preach' and it was so much fun! I still have the tape!"

So we made our way down the midway, over the straw covered path, past the din of the Tilt-A-Whirl and the nursery-rhyme strains of the carousel, past the ring-toss and the fun-house and the water rifle shoot, until we heard the pop music echoing out of a tiny booth.

StarStruck. It was blue, covered with silver stars, just like I remembered. The gateway to a real studio. To stardom.

"You're sure you want to do this?"

"Yes, Dad! Geez!"

The pimply-faced teen working the front took me into the booth and handed me off to his co-worker inside the sound booth.

"So whatcha wannna sing?"

"'Wind Beneath My Wings,'" I said, confidently.

"O-kaay," he said, handing me a set of headphones. "So, what we'll do is play it once so you can practice, then we play it again and record. Got it?"

"Yep." I had done this before. Piece of cake. I put the

headphones on and stepped up to the mike. Just like a real star. Just like I would do all the time when somebody discovered me. I wonder how I would manage concerts and school? Surely we could figure out a way to —

Bette Midler poured into my headphones, beginning the song with a long, "Oh, oh, oh, oh," that I hadn't remembered. Had it always gone up and down like that?

I began to sing along and realized that while I knew the words to the chorus, I hadn't the slightest clue about the verses. And there were no lyrics anywhere, just Bette in the headphones.

But it was fine. I had this round for practice.

Then I noticed the guy working the equipment laughing, and the funnel cake began to swirl in my stomach.

About 10 seconds after the practice round was over, the music started again and the equipment guy yelled, "Taping this time!"

I swallowed, pushing down stage fright for an audience that wasn't there.

"Did you ever know that you're my hero, you're everything I wish I could be ..."

My voice was shaking. Maybe *this* was how stars got that vibrato thing!

Bette was getting louder, and I closed my eyes, pretending the microphone was my hairbrush, and held nothing back. "Fly, fly, fly high against the sky, so high I almost touched the sky. Thank you, thank you, thank God for you, the wind beneath my wings."

The equipment guy was grinning broadly, revealing a

set of teeth so crooked they looked British. "We'll have your tape ready in a few minutes," he said.

"Ok, so, do I just get it out front?"

"Yeah, after they play it."

"You mean, like, in here?"

"No, girlie. They play it out on the midway for everybody to hear. Then you'll get your tape." He grinned again, and I felt my deodorant fail.

"Can't you just give it to me without playing it?"

"Nope."

"Come on, why not? I'll just take it."

"We gotta make sure there's nothin wrong with it, don't we?"

My father was still on the midway, parked on a bench squarely in front of the StarStruck booth. He sipped a Coke and grinned.

"How was it?"

"Great. Can we, um, just, go over there?" I gestured wildly down the straw strewn path to the arcade games.

"Don't you have to get your tape?"

"Yeah, but Dad, they're gonna play it! Out here, in front of everybody!"

"You don't know any of these people," he said, taking another sip of Coke. "Come on, just sit. It'll be fine. Besides, I'm sure you were great."

I sat, slouching, looking at my white Keds, until a voice came over the loudspeaker. It was a crisp day, but suddenly even my hair was sweating.

"Ladies and gentlemen, please feast your ears on this! It's ... MICHELLE, singing Cher's 'If I Could Turn

Back Time.'"

When the music started, I was frozen. It was blaring. So loud you couldn't *not* hear it. Michelle sounded like she could win Star Search. Her voice was rich and throaty, just like Cher, and what's more, she knew all the words.

"Dad, seriously, can't we just go down there a little ways? Please?" I pulled at his arm.

"No, we'll never find a place to sit down there. Just wait a minute and we'll go play whatever it is you want to play."

"No, Dad, it's not that, it's that I don't want to —"

"And now!" boomed the pimply faced kid. "You're in for a special treat, all right! Here's ANGIE, singing Bette Midler's 'Wind Beneath My Wings!'"

Ohmigod.

That voice couldn't possibly be mine. I didn't sound like that. This strange voice was weak and tinny and painfully out of tune.

Beside me, my father was laughing. When the voice reached the first chorus, he'd gotten to his full belly laugh, the one that raised his voice up to a falsetto.

A group of men strolling down the midway stopped in front of the StarStruck booth. One of them leaned over, put his hands on his knees, and started to howl like a dog. The rest joined him--a pack howling men in jeans-shorts, flip flops, wife-beaters, and baseball caps. Their pack drew more people, many right in front of our bench.

"My ears! I think I've gone deaf!"

"Lawdy, somebody make it stop!"

"She's got to be, like, the worst singer on the entire planet."

"Damn, if my dog were here he'd be howlin' at that just like them boys over there."

The song crescendoed into my grand finale, and my father, who had never stopped laughing, was now crying.

"Turn it off!" someone yelled from the crowd. "Please, turn it off!"

Finally, it ended, and they called me over the loudspeaker to come pick up my tape.

"Dad," I pleaded, "please go get it for me. Please."

"Aww, sugar," he put an arm around me. "Don't cry."

"Please, can you just go get it?" I whispered.

"Sure."

Back home, my mother and sister were watching TV.

"How was the State Fair?" my mom asked.

"You won't believe what she did," Dad said, grabbing the tape out of my hands.

"Dad, no! Give that back!"

"She did that StarStruck thing again. You've gotta hear it. It's so bad guys were howling like dogs when they played it on the midway." He muted the TV and put the tape in the cassette player.

And then it happened again.

They all doubled over laughing, and this time, I cried.

"It's not funny!" I said, when the tape was over.

"You really thought you could sing?" my sister asked. "Seriously? You're like, the worst singer ever."

I clenched the plastic of the tape casing in my fist.

"I know that. Now."

In my room I took the tape and pulled out its shiny black guts, farther and farther until they curled onto the floor like ringlets. But somebody could still take a pencil to it, if they really wanted to. So I pulled the ends, hard, until they came loose from the cassette, and then grabbed a pair of scissors and cut the black ribbon of shame, over and over, until nothing remained but tiny pieces.

THE CALENDAR
MELISSA RUTLEDGE KIRTLEY

I'll draw it perfectly, I thought. I used a ruler to draw the lines perfectly straight. I sharpened my pencil after making each line in the grid.

I re-measured each of the squares. They were all exactly one inch by one inch. With my best penmanship, I wrote in the numbers. I used the ruler again to make sure each number was the same size and in the same location as the number in the previous square.

Mom had been going out a lot lately, leaving me and my brother home alone. Being the older sibling by eleven years meant that I was always in charge. If I heard the term "built-in babysitter" one more time, I would scream.

When she sees how much effort I put into this, she'll know how important this is to me. I hushed the voice in my head that told me to quit dreaming. My heart didn't want to hear it, even if it already knew the truth.

I wrote the month across the top of the page, lightly at first so I could erase it if it was off-center. Then I darkened the letters once I had it just right.

"February."

Each letter was evenly spaced, but the tail on the "y" dipped below the line a little too much. I made a small, gray smudge on the page when I erased it. Dammit. A blemish on my otherwise flawless calendar. I considered crumbling up the paper and starting over for a third time, but decided against it. She might not even notice the smudge.

I imagined how the conversation would go. I would hand my mother the calendar without saying a word. She would look at it, unsure of what she was seeing at first. Then she would realize what it was, and a small "Oh no," would escape her lips. Her hand would go to her heart, and her eyes would wet with tears. She would open her arms to me and say "I'm so sorry, sweetie. I didn't realize."

I would hug her back and say, "It's okay," and then everything would be better.

The voice in my head guffawed and interrupted my daydream with a sarcastic, "Yeah, right!"

I just have to show her and make her see, my heart replied. *If I just show her, I can fix this.*

I filled in the calendar, marking the days she went out and left us alone. In the last two weeks, Mom had gone out with her boyfriend on nine of the days. Except when they went out last Friday night, and she didn't come home until Monday morning before she went to work. So technically that made eleven days.

At almost sixteen years old, I could easily take care of myself and my four year old brother, Aaron. I could make us dinner and play video games with him until bedtime. Mom's boyfriend had recently bought us a used Super Nintendo game system, and Aaron and I would play Super Mario World until our thumbs were sore. Even though I let him stay up way past his bedtime, he always went to bed hours before Mom came home. That is, if she came home instead of sleeping over at *his* house.

I helped Aaron brush his teeth and put on his pajamas. I read him his bedtime stories and sang him to sleep. We would lie in Mom's bed together after the lights were out, and I would sing "Cherish," that old song from the 60s by The Association. Aaron would lay his head on my shoulder, and I would stroke his hair and his face. His small body snuggled up against mine made it easy to forgive his earlier tantrums of the day. Once I felt his breath become slow and even, I would quietly slip out of the room and do my homework before going to bed.

Sometimes Aaron would wake up and call out for Mom, and I would go back in and sing to him some more. Eventually, he started calling out for me instead of her.

Since meeting her boyfriend, Mom went out more nights than she stayed home. When she did stay home, either she talked to him on the phone for hours or he came over to our house.

After several months of this, I decided to make the calendar. My friends had stopped asking me to hang out because I declined so many invitations. "I can't go. I have to babysit." My friendships grew weaker and weaker every time I said it. That super annoying girl, Jenny, replaced me in our group. She now sat in the front seat of Beth's car and went to her house after school. I wanted my mom back and my friends back, too.

I loved my baby brother. I ached for him. It wasn't his fault that Dad left and Mom had a new life that we didn't fit into. Aaron didn't understand what was happening, but I began to resent him anyway. His confusion, sadness and anger made his behavior unruly. Everything was a fight. I didn't want to cook him dinner anymore. I hated arguing with him about turning off the video game. I dreaded the bedtime battle every night.

He's not my kid! I wanted to scream as I filled in the calendar. I felt my cheeks get hot and my heart start to pound. I took deep breaths and reminded myself that she couldn't see me angry. Mom made it very clear that only *she* had a right to be angry. Instead, I needed to let my wall down and allow her see my pain. Once she saw it, I knew she would listen.

No mother wants to see her child hurting, said my heart. The voice in my head was not convinced.

I placed the calendar under my algebra book to keep it hidden and pristine. I went to sleep with a plan in my head, replaying our conversation over and over.

In the weeks that followed, I recorded more of Mom's evenings out until the month was over. The time had arrived to show the calendar to her, but fear allowed me to keep putting it off.

"MELISSA MAE!"

When I heard Mom scream my name in that tone, my insides froze and I instantly knew what happened. She found the calendar.

Nooooo! I thought and closed my eyes. *This isn't how it was supposed to go!* Our small house and my whole body trembled and she stomped into the kitchen where I remained paralyzed.

"What is *this*?" Mom had a way of hissing and yelling at the same time. Without waiting for an answer, she shook the paper in my face and continued. "How *dare* you track where I go and what I do! What did you plan on doing with this? Were you going to show it to *your dad*?" She said his name with a venom reserved only for him.

"No, I wasn't. I promise. I was just going to show you, that's all ..." I started to explain, but she didn't let me finish.

"Oh, yeah right!" That famous contemptuous look overcame her face, the one that instantly reduced me down to nothing. Feeling small and worthless, I couldn't meet my mother's infuriated gaze. She ripped the calendar into shreds. My meticulous work fell to the floor in pieces.

"Did you think I was going to feel *bad* for you?" she asked. I didn't answer. "Oh, poor Melissa. Her life is so hard." Her mocking punched me in my chest. The calendar had been a stupid idea. My heart swelled with regret as it sank.

Told you so, said the voice in my head.

"You think you can control me? Now that I finally have a life, you want to take it away? You are so *selfish*, just like *your father* ..."

Her tantrum went on for several minutes. I stopped listening and rebuilt the walls around my heart. My mother's hatred washed over me, carrying with it the realization that my needs did not matter. Her need for a man in her life superseded my needs: to have a mom, and to not be a mother-figure to my brother.

Defeat replaced hope, and a numb acceptance settled in my soul. I vowed she would never see my pain again, and the best way to ensure that was to not feel anything.

Someday I will matter to someone, my heart promised. The voice in my head pitied me and stayed quiet.

I created a new calendar, though I never drew it on paper. I waited, mentally marking red X's through the passing days until I could make my escape.

Four years later, I boarded a plane for California and never looked back.

GOOD ENOUGH
TRACY RIMDZIUS

The smug look on my sanctimonious hallmate's face said, "I have this covered," as we all prepared to reveal our Purity Test scores.

Not so fast, sweetheart. You have a boyfriend. I'm practically a bar of Ivory soap over here.

All eyes on me, I announced my score last. I focused on the only positive aspect of reaching college with this much purity intact, spoiling her victory.

"96."

The others exchanged some glances, and I shrugged. *It takes two to tango, people.* I definitely had someone in mind.

I fell for him almost immediately the night he performed card tricks for me. He swept in claiming I would be amazed. But I watched without seeing the tricks, transfixed instead by how his eyes sparkled with the promise of laughter.

"Well?" He asked after each trick.

"It was OK," I teased. We clicked immediately into playful banter.

We saw each other every day. We shared our favorite music. We sang together loudly. We sat up half the night talking. I could not hear him laugh without laughing myself. Our marathon of smiling made my face ache.

Alcohol plying us, we lay in his bed one night. He stole the pillow from under my head. "I hate you," I said in mock complaint.

He ran his fingers through my tangle of curls. "You don't hate me."

Our sudden closeness was too much and not enough. Overwhelmed, I closed my eyes. I felt his arm slip around me, and his hand on mine.

"You're being boring," he dared.

When I opened my eyes, I found his locked on me. Frozen with anticipation, I waited for my first kiss. It would not come from him.

The older guys on the hall had supplied the alcohol. They felt like big brothers and many nights I shuffled over to their suite in slippers and pajamas to hang out. One day a new face was there, a friend of one of them. He sat quietly in the corner, mostly observing. He upset the balance somehow.

We all planned to go to a party. I dressed in my early 90s finest: tapered black knit pants, loose green silk blouse, and black blazer with the patch on the front pocket. The guys never commented on my appearance, but that night they kept saying how nice I looked.

The boy I loved came in and announced he wasn't going to the party. I no longer wanted to go either, but I heard *her* voice drifting in from the hallway. My friends asked, "Hey, are you coming?"

I watched the boy I loved leave to spend the evening with someone else and resigned myself. "Yeah, I'm coming."

The crush of people made me want to leave the party immediately. At the bar, the new guy kept talking to me and I could not mask my surprise. He looked as bored as me. "This party is over. Let's go. Should we get the others?" He seemed to be testing me.

I just wanted to leave. "It's up to you."

We walked alone back to my room. He led me on a path that was longer than necessary, but I was relieved to breathe fresh air. He commented on our drunkenness, but I'd nursed the same beer all night. We'd never really spoken before and it suddenly felt very important that he understand his mistake. I tried to convince him I was sober.

"I don't think you would be so friendly if you were sober."

Great, I'm unfriendly.

He wanted to talk to me when we got back to my room. I agreed. But when he closed the door behind us, I felt sealed off from everything. When I told him he could turn on the light, he lowered his voice. "I like the dark."

Jesus, really? I had to bite my tongue to stop myself from laughing. But I didn't turn on the light. The darkness made him brave. It made me stiff and unsure.

He asked if he could sit next to me on my bed. I could feel him watching me, but I stared straight ahead. As our eyes adjusted to the dark, he looked around my room. "You can tell a lot about a person from their room."

I glanced at my homemade collage made of magazine clippings, beanbag chair, and favorite teddy bear. *Uh-oh.*

"You are sophisticated. But I can also tell that by the way you dress and act."

I can tell you are full of shit.

When I didn't respond, he went on. "At the risk of sounding like one of the boys, you really do look nice tonight."

I created silence. The less I spoke, the harder it became to speak. He kept breaking the silence. "This is weird. I never thought I would be in your room talking to you."

That makes two of us, Buddy. Though naïve, I could still recognize his attempt to throw out lines, to see if any would catch me. But I didn't care. At least something was actually happening to me.

Voices came in from the hallway. I leaned away from him and strained to hear them, grateful for the distraction. I just needed a second to think.

He started rubbing my ring finger. The novelty of even that slight touch almost made me jump. But I kept perfectly still. He pulled his hand away and laughed. "You are too smart to play games with. I've never done

17

this before ... can I kiss you?"

I was as shocked as if he'd slapped me. I finally looked at him. *How long do I have to think about it? Hmm, not this long.*

I didn't want to say yes, but I couldn't say no. "I don't know."

The kiss persisted for what seemed like forever and the whole time I continued debating whether I wanted to participate. *At least he'll figure out this sucks and won't be interested anymore.*

But he wouldn't give up and I had to pull away. I leaned on his shoulder to avoid looking at him.

"How was it?"

Oh my God, he can't be serious!

I threw it back at him. "What did *you* think?"

"It wasn't bad."

This time, I couldn't help laughing. *How did I get myself into this?*

He flinched. "Why are you laughing at me?"

How does he not know? "I'm laughing at myself."

"Can I try again?"

I shook my head. *There's no way I'd be any better at it.*

He sighed. "It's going to be awkward next time we see each other, isn't it?"

You are so drunk you'll never remember this. "Why does it have to be?"

He stayed quiet so long I stopped expecting an answer. He surprised me when he started to speak. "Well, you know now that I find you attractive, and the feeling is not mutual."

But I didn't really know what I thought and I said so. He wanted more of an explanation but I couldn't elaborate. I asked him to leave instead.

When I said, "Good night," he came back and kissed me on the forehead.

"Sweet dreams."

I lay down on the floor and waited to feel something. Tears came instead. I think I already knew I would settle for him.

TIPPING POINT
ERIN MARGOLIN

In college I fell in love with a girl named Ellen. I first met her as she bounded up a creaky staircase, racing into our Women's Studies class in the old John Stone House. She was wearing a t-shirt and jeans, and her cheeks were pink like cotton candy. She plopped down in the only empty seat left, which was right next to me, because she was ten minutes late. Something made me freeze, and I held my breath so the grits I'd had for breakfast wouldn't waft her way. She sat so close I could smell her shampoo, and her still damp hair had left a wet spot on the back of her shirt. After a few minutes I started stealing glances at her. She caught me once. I looked at my lap as my face grew blotchy and warm. I fiddled with a loose thread on my pants and pretended to take notes, ignoring my heart thumping in my chest.

I couldn't stop thinking about her. Dancing through

my every daydream, the object of my obsessions, she was oblivious to the pedestal I'd placed her upon. Tucked into a small corner at my favorite coffee shop, I journaled about her while watching cars go by on Old Canton Road. I helped myself to a red Solo cup full of something lethal on Fraternity Row Thursday nights, trying to distract myself, trying to figure out what I wanted and if I'd ever have the balls to talk to her. I lied in bed at night waiting, wondering and twisting the corner of my purple sheet. Faces of boys I'd dated floated through my mind, memories of making out and fooling around in cars … but Ellen was foreign territory. My insides clenched up and I tossed and turned. Sleep eluded me.

After a few weeks I sent Ellen an email. To my surprise and delight, she responded and we became fast friends. We preferred writing to face-to-face interactions, perhaps because of my social ineptitude and our shared shyness. I was fidgety and scared around her. She was, too, although she didn't admit it. But I noticed it whenever we were together. So we connected through a computer screen.

The emails flew between us, some just saying a quick hello, while others were diatribes ending with *"I miss you."* We had so much to talk about, it seemed. Messages became intensely personal, and some days I moved around in a fog, thick like split pea soup. I confided in her about everything, and she me. I analyzed her every word. Over the summer we wrote letters back and forth, many were eight or ten pages long. Written *by hand.* I saved hers in an old Bass shoebox that I hid under my bed.

I knew feeling things for Ellen was unusual. I couldn't ignore it anymore, but I didn't dare say anything to her. To anyone. I could barely admit to myself what was carved upon my heart and surely visible to everyone else. What made it harder is that I started to sense she had feelings for me, too.

Desperately seeking validation, I headed to my shrink's office. It was Dr. Smith's job to have an objective opinion. I brought Ellen's letters in my backpack along with a scrapbook she'd made me. The inside covers of it were peppered with hundreds of pictures of flowers she'd cut by hand out of magazines and glued into place — like the walls of Idgie Threadgood's room in the old folks' home in Fried Green Tomatoes, one of my favorite movies. In my mind, we were Idgie and Ruth. Dr. Smith opened the scrapbook and her mouth fell open. She covered it with her hand as thumbed through the pages. I sat on my hands waiting for my sentence, waiting for the guillotine to come down, shiny and flashing, to prove that I was nothing but a crazy, fucked up college kid.

My last piece of evidence for Dr. Smith was a particular card from Ellen. It stood out from all the others, and I read portions of it aloud as tears ran down my cheeks. I didn't need to read it because I'd gone over it so many times I knew the words by heart. Over Spring Break Ellen had gone to California with some girlfriends while I'd gone home to visit family. Inside, she'd begun writing:

Dear Doodlebug,

Everyone else is outside on the patio drinking, talking and laughing. But all I can do is think about you and wonder what you're doing And I'm getting that shaky feeling inside because I know you can't possibly be missing me as much. I love you. You make my heart hurt.

Only I *was* missing her just as much. Reading those words was the tipping point for me; that single card convinced me she felt the same. I couldn't keep everything inside much longer, but a part of me continued to doubt my instincts. Until Dr. Smith weighed in.

She looked right at me and said, "I don't need to see anymore. This girl clearly has feelings for you." Dr. Smith told me it was time to tell Ellen what was going on inside my head.

Later that night I asked Ellen to meet me in one of the lecture halls so we could talk privately. It was quiet and empty, so different from during the day. Darker. Things echoed. We sat next to each other on the steps leading down to the stage. My heart thudded in my chest and I didn't think I could do it. Somehow I did. I don't remember anything I said that night except that at some point I whispered (while looking down at my white wigwam socks and Doc Martens—not at her, no eye contact), *"Sometimes I want to kiss you,"* and then I lost it and started choking on sobs. I put my elbows on my knees and cradled my head inside the cave of my torso. I wanted to disappear.

Ellen was calm, rational, and businesslike. She turned everything upside down and talked me out of it. She insisted I was feeling our friendship very deeply and that we were just really connected and in tune with one another. Ellen made it seem so simple and told me to stop over thinking things. Soon I was apologizing, she hugged me and it was all over. A quick flash, a zip of lightning; the truth zoomed across the sky and smashed me into a million pieces.

I bought into her arguments, I clung to them. Because I had no choice in that moment. But after that, I hated myself. Although I'd told her everything and didn't have to hide anymore, I felt exposed, stupid, and betrayed.

Within days I became a zombie. I stopped sleeping, eating, and I didn't want to leave my bed.

So I made a plan. I needed a physical pain to take the place of the emotional pain. I needed a distraction to feel whole again.

I calmly took a shower, washed and conditioned my hair, inhaling the scent of my Herbal Essence shampoo. I lathered every inch of myself, scrubbing hard. I shaved my legs. I rinsed. I got out, toweled off, and put on my favorite t-shirt and sweatpants. With my wet hair hanging down my back, I returned to the bathroom. My suitemates were watching television and laughing.

I was invisible. It was perfect. My pain called out, begging me to unleash it.

I quietly closed the doors to the bathroom. I picked

up my razor and put on a fresh blade.

I knelt over the drain so I wouldn't make a mess. And I slashed my left wrist.

The bright red blood came quickly to the surface. I heaved a sigh, then cut again, slightly lower, and gritted my teeth. More blood oozed up. It hurt but was a release at the same time. I was dumb. I made the whole thing up inside my head. Or did I? I recalled the time she'd gone around campus picking me wildflowers. I cut again and again, punishing myself and begging my anguish and memories to recede as a result of this bloodletting.

I didn't know what was true anymore. I loved her. She loved me, too. Or I was just losing my mind? What the fuck was wrong with me? With **HER?**

A long strand of mucous hung from my nose and I realized I was crying. The snot plopped down in the middle of all that blood.

I started to laugh. But there was crying mixed in. Maybe it was hysteria.

A door opened and my roommate's voice came, "What are you doing ..." and she trailed off into a hissing and went running for the phone. My suitemate came and gently took my razor from me.

I leaned against the cool tiles, all wet hair, snot, tears, and blood.

I felt holy. I was real again.

OF GREAT PERIL
JULIA A. MAKI

Prec·i·pice/ˈprɛsəpɪs/ [pres-uh-pis]

1. (noun) The brink of a dangerous or
   disastrous situation.
2. a situation of great peril: on the
   precipice of war.

Unidentified shapes blurred together in shades of
green and gray across the scope — soft and whimsical,
like a Monet. I became entranced by the swirls and
colors of the cloud layers blending as one. I had been
staring at the vortex for so long now; my mind began
drifting off to memories of home. The little farmhouse
on a hill that I grew up in was surrounded by rolling
fields, a lake that rarely caught a ripple from the wind,

and tree-covered mountains that broke jaggedly along the horizon. I could almost smell the scent of morning rain that seeped from the branches of the evergreens. The mountains cast a solitude that would almost magically recharge my soul and strained muscles during my few visits home.

My mind had been going back to these familiar places of tranquility quite often now — especially when the missions drug into their painful 5th or 6th hour of flight. Though it was an imaginary land up here — free of trivial burdens — the long days sucked any trace of energy we had left in our bones.

Suddenly I was shaken out of daydreams and back into reality. The images on the display began to jolt up and down as the ride took a nauseating turn. I attempted to control the stick and override the constantly changing altitude of the aircraft with each air pocket. "Yanking and banking" they liked to call it. The plane shook ferociously and I began to wonder if every bolt that was holding it together would simultaneously vibrate loose.

"Hey Knuckles, you see anything yet?" A familiar voice called over the ICS (internal radio).

"Not yet, sir," I said, secretly rolling my eyes. "Why don't you try flying straight and level for awhile?" I said, blaming him for the air pockets. It's just what we did. There was no escaping friendly torment from the crew no matter who you were.

"Hey, why don't you just do your job and let me do mine?" he joked, his Long Island accent slipping in sporadically. "I'll worry about the plane and keeping your sorry ass alive —"

"Wait — wait!" I interrupted him- though I was disappointed I wouldn't get to hear his lame defense. In all fairness, he was one of the best pilots I'd ever flown with — which made it even more satisfying and acceptable to rip on his flying abilities. When it came down to a 'hot and heavy' moment of combat, I wouldn't have trusted my life with any other. Every day he held each of our lives in his hands. Time and time again he proved that he was up for the job.

"I think I have something here," I exclaimed. "Hold it. Steady. Right here ..." I focused the lens in and out trying to get a clear picture of the land thousands of feet below me. "Damn! Stupid friggin' clouds are in the way again."

The clouds drifted in and blanketed my lens, as if they had not a care in the world that they were interrupting important military orders. "We're gonna have to circle around again."

"Roger. Circling." As he said it, the pilot cranked the rudder hard to the left. He always chose left if there was the option. His visibility was better that way, as being the (PPC) Patrol Plane Captain, he always sat in the left seat, unless he was instructing a junior pilot.

The plane whined and protested, showing its age. It resisted the sharp angle as long as it could, but the pilot was still able to out-muscle the four engines. The Earth's gravitational pull crushed my ribs into the counsel as he jerked the plane over hard. I felt my lunch come up to my throat, and swallowed hard to keep it from coming any further. The blood in my brain rushed to my feet and it became a struggle to hold my head up from the weight of the invisible Gs that pressed it downward. It's amazing that a person can get used to this unnatural feeling and ward off puking by sheer willpower.

"I can't believe it. What a bunch of crap." I began to put a voice to my thoughts, filling the dead air time. I hated long silences. "We have the technology to see someone light a cigarette from 25,000 feet, but throw a little cloud in there and we're about as useless as nipples on a bull." On days like this I had a hard time believing we were the world's most powerful Navy when our equipment had such an easy fail-rate. I'm sure Congress would argue that the tax-payer's money was better off invested in their retirement funds and beach houses instead of new military equipment.

"Alright, kid. We're coming back into the hotspot. Are you getting anything yet?" asked the voice from the flight station. The plane leveled out and I pressed my thumb into the controller for the camera, leaving an imprint in my skin.

All I could make out was a ghostly haze penetrating everywhere, protecting secrets and laughing at our fumbling efforts. In a matter of minutes, it began to break up and flashes of the ground came into view. At last, the final pieces of clouds trickled off of the wingtips like melting butter. "Okay, hold it. Steady ... a few degrees higher ... and there it is ..." My feelings of satisfaction of accomplishing the mission were quickly replaced by a repulsive sickness in my stomach. As my camera locked onto the target, my voice trailed off and I gasped, feeling the air leave my lungs. I was paralyzed.

"What is it?" beckoned the voice on the radio.

Talk to him, I thought. *Tell him. What are you waiting for?* I realized that I had never thought about what it would actually look like when we found it.

"Talk to me, Knuckles. What are you looking at?"

"This is the place they briefed. We found it ... It's right here." My voice sounded disembodied. It was no longer my own. It was coming from somewhere far away.

"Quick — go ahead and begin annotation. Tell me, what do you see?" His voice was filled with urgency.

I snapped the record switch down into the "on" position. "Well," I began. *Take a breath and just talk.* "I'm — a.. I'm imaging the slope of the mountain and following it with the camera to where it intersects on the ground with its neighboring mountain. They are very dull and weathered. Grey and spurts of dead grass. Not a lot of rocky edges; you know, like they've been around for awhile. Between the mountains, there is a valley with a small ... canyon. But it looks like it could be partially man-made. I'm not sure. There's white stuff inside but it's too low in the valley to be snow." I stared at the mountainside. *They looked just like **my** mountains* — yet it was a world away.

"White stuff?" He cleared his throat. "What kind of white stuff?"

"Hold on a minute ... Let me get it focused ... Oh god."

"What? What is it?!" He was almost shouting now.

The realization flooded over me like a pail of ice water in my face.

"Al, they're ..." I swallowed and stared at the color of flesh that was revealed under the tattered cloths. "It's them." *Don't panic. This is what you do. This is your job.* "They're piled everywhere and it looks like they tried to cover them in sheets or powder or something. At first it looked like snow ... or stacks ... of flour. But then you can see- where some of the sheets are torn away — you can see what's underneath." I knew I was still being recorded. Did I sound unprofessional? I no longer cared.

The tip of my thumbnail snapped back from the pressure on the controller. I didn't notice the pain.

"Knuckles? You alright, man?"

I waited until I felt that my breath was normal again before I answered him. This time in a near whisper.

"Yeah, yeah, I'm here."

"Need a break?"

"Nope. I'm fine ... Just getting this all on tape. I see some birds down there moving around all over. Other than that it's very ... still." I don't know what I expected from a mass gravesite.

I wanted to go home. They couldn't pretend it didn't exist anymore.

My walks through the mountains no longer bring me the comfort they used to. From a distance, most mountain ranges look strikingly similar.

No one remembers Bosnia and Kosovo anymore. It has been long overshadowed by Iraq and Afghanistan. Honestly, I wish I could forget it too.

APPLE PIE THERAPY
KIM SISTO ROBINSON

{ Dedicated to my dear sister, Kay, who was murdered by her husband on May 26, 2010. The world darkened & shook on that day.}

Four words, which have abundantly annoyed me since my sister's murder are:

It. Will. Get. Better.

I ask you kindly to please suck those thoughtless, naive words back into your ignorant throat.

Unless, of course, your soul mate, root of your root, and blood of your blood has been executed, too.

Only then might I consider listening to your counsel. Only then will I know you in fact understand and empathize with one who exists with a partial heart.

It's been hell on earth.

Triple fucking hell if you want the whole truth.

But I've stumbled upon certain activities to distract me in the midst of my sorrow, to divert me from my insanity.

What a relief — when one can take a break from being crazy.

What a release — when one can be removed temporarily from suffering.

For example, the day before my birthday, my friend, Tia, calls.

"Clear your day tomorrow morning. I'm teaching you how to make apple pies."

It is not a request.

I arrive at her house at 9:00 a.m. on October 4th.

She already has the centers organized and prearranged skillfully: the apple peeling center, the crust making center, the sugar and butter center.

She claps her hands together.

"Okay, how about a Margarita before we begin?"

"Um, it's like, 9:05 in the morning. Are you serious?"

"Believe me," she smiles. "You need A LOT of booze."

I giggle at that. Nothing could be more true.

"Well, it's 5:00 in Kenya. Why the hell not."

We sip slowly and gossip voraciously about Project Runway, husbands, kids, our jobs.

We begin getting serious about apples at 10:00.

Tia has one of those incredible apple peeling gadgets. I don't know what they're called, but there's something abundantly comforting about watching the skin of the apple unravel and shed its body to the tiled floor.

Kind of like something surprising might be exposed in the end.

And although the apple skinning is therapeutic and healing, nothing compares to preparing the crust.

Measuring. Sifting. Cutting in shortening. Mixing.

Ahhh.

Then the wrapping of hands around the soft pillow of dough.

Big fat Buddha tummy.

"Don't be afraid of it," Tia says. "Pound it. Pretend it's the murderer."

I make a fist and pound the dough with all my strength.

"Take that, you bastard," I screech.

I punch it harder harder harder.

"That's what you get, you murdering son of a bitch!"

"Hey, let me help," Tia shouts, bumping into my behind.

We both begin thumping the hell out to the dough.

If somebody peeked through the window, I suspect they'd call the funny farm immediately.

"You better quite your day job teaching English," I say. "I hear they're hiring a boxing instructor at the high school."

"Ha ha ha," Tia says.

After that, silence fills the kitchen like a black water flowing, like a Platholian poem pouring.

"Oh, God, why didn't we do something?" I bellow. "Why didn't we break his legs so he couldn't walk? Why didn't we fracture his fingers so he couldn't pick up a gun? Why why why?"

"I know," Tia cries. "She should be here baking pies with us. She. Should. Be. Here."

We sit without words for a long time.

Lady Antebellum plays in the background.

The clock ticks slowly, unhurriedly.

I hate that insidious clock.

How can it tick when Kay is dead at Oneonta Cemetery?

How can my legs move, my eyes see?

How can my heart beat?

Suddenly, Tia jumps out of her chair scaring the daylights out of me.

"SHIT!" She screams. "We still have apple crisp to make, Kimmers!"

She throws flour in my face, waits for a response.

We begin laughing unexpectedly, beautifully. We link our arms together and begin dancing and twirling to Lady Antebellum's, "I Need You. "

It comes out of nowhere like a soft glimmer of light

Like a small prayer.

And I can almost hear Kay laughing, too. Snorting that famous, comical snort of hers.

Almost.

Sometimes all you need is a good girlfriend, two or three strawberry margaritas, and love love love.

Sometimes all you truly need is the interruption of apples, flour, and cinnamon to survive.

One. More. Day.

PREPARE A PLACE FOR ME
JANICE WILBERG

There was only one reason why my father would be calling me. My mother must be dead.

He explained how it happened, how just last week he had given up taking care of her at home, that for the third time, she'd gone limp in the bathtub and he'd had to call the fire department to come lift her and take her to the cherry wood bed they'd bought as newlyweds 64 years before. He apologized to me. If he hadn't been holding their ancient wall phone, he would have been wringing his hands. She had only lived a week in the Alzheimer's Unit and he had visited every night, he said, taking tapes of the music he thought she would remember and playing it on the ancient Press Play tape player they kept in the basement.

He was sure she still knew him. He told me how she had kissed his hands when they last said goodbye. She had taken both of his hands in hers and kissed his hands. I couldn't imagine it. It was my mother whose hands would be kissed. It was my mother's impossibly soft cheek and the smell of her face powder and English Lavender soap that drew us to her seeking the blessing of kissing her. Alzheimer's had changed a lot about her.

The realization that I was, temporarily at least, sibling in charge hit me hard after I got through Chicago traffic and on to the smooth raceway across western Michigan that is I-96, mile after mile of rolling countryside with no interruptions except the tiny roadside wineries giving free shots to interstate drivers. I found every possible reason to delay. I sampled the wine, hunted for snacks at massive truck stops, and even pulled over to check the old Michigan map to make sure I hadn't suddenly forgotten how to drive home. What was I thinking being the first responder on the scene of a catastrophe? That was my brother's job. I stalled as long as I could, going the speed limit and not a mile faster, but eventually I made it to my folks' driveway and within thirty seconds, my dad was standing at the screen door.

"Thanks for coming, Janice," he said, like I was the last guest to leave a dull party. To add to the oddness of the night, my father then hugged me. I was 53. My father must have hugged me before this night, but I don't remember it ever happening. So when my father hugged me, I told him I needed to go to the drugstore right away. "What do you need? We probably have whatever you need here," he said.

"I need to buy make up, Dad. I left home without my

make up. So I need to go to the drugstore and buy stuff, you know, like mascara," I answered. Barely having put my keys down on the table, I grabbed them back up and started toward the door. "I'll be back in 15 minutes." As I walked out the door, I heard the familiar screech as he pulled the lever to bring up the footrest on his La-Z-Boy rocker. He was sitting in his chair where he belonged, I thought. In a minute, he'll turn the TV on and resume watching CNN with the sound muted and then he'll pick up the book on top of the stack next to his chair and start reading where he left off when he'd heard my car in the driveway. I knew exactly what he was doing. I felt relieved that he was doing what he always did. He wasn't crying or hugging me. He was being himself.

The drug store had that fluorescent weird feeling that all stores have when it's eleven o'clock at night and no one is there except the girl working the check-out and the guy in back restocking the Fritos. I walked up and down the cosmetics department. L'Oreal, Maybelline, Max Factor. I stuck at Maybelline for a long minute looking at the mascara and wondering if they still made the little red plastic boxes with the tiny brush and bar of dark color that required a little squirt of spit to moisten. I remembered the little box in the right hand drawer of the cherry wood vanity, sitting atop an embroidered guest towel that my mother used as a drawer liner, and next to the mascara box was the eyebrow pencil she used on her beautiful, business-like eyebrows, and, sometimes, to give herself a beauty mark low on her right cheek. In the evenings, she would sit at her vanity table with the small lamp casting a yellow light in the darkness of her room, a place so serene and cool and off-limits, and she would paint her nails red leaving perfectly lined half-moons. She was as ephemeral a person as ever lived on this earth and she was not going to be there when I went home. Was she?

We talked about my mother's funeral. "Whatever you think is right, Dad," I kept answering whenever he asked what to do. Should we have a graveside service or a full-fledged funeral? My father, one practiced at snap and sometimes life-changing decision-making, was clearly stuck. For the first time in his 88 years, he was indecisive.

"John thinks we should just go with the graveside service. Not that many people would come to a service at the funeral home. Do you think that's right?" He had just hung up the phone after the third or fourth phone conversation about this topic with my brother, stuck in bad weather across the country.

"I think that's fine, Dad." I didn't really think it was fine. My mother deserved the whole funeral shebang. Plenty of people knew her and liked her. I didn't want anything about her funeral being quick or cheap. I held my tongue. I had been estranged from my parents for ten years until just a year ago. It wasn't my place, I thought, to have an opinion.

We picked out a casket together and the clothes that my mother would wear. I took off my pearl earrings and asked the funeral director to put them on my mother along with the locket my dad had given her 65 years before when they were engaged. Later I drove back to the funeral home to make sure they knew to curl my mother's hair. In her Alzheimer's fog, she had taken to wearing a baseball cap over her straight hair. My father may have remembered her curled hair but he couldn't do anything about it.

Dozens of people came to her wake. My father stood in the center of the large room, my mother lying in her open casket off to the side, and he talked to everyone as if he was hosting a cocktail party. He talked about golf and bowling, two things they had done together. He greeted former employees from their Ben Franklin store and listened to their stories about how wonderful and kind my mother had been to them. He looked toward the door every few minutes to see if my brother was there. But he never showed, still stuck in in Oregon.

I prepared for my brother not being there the next day when we would follow the hearse 90 miles to her hometown and bury her next to her parents on a hill in the cemetery where, during our estrangement, I had seen their headstones already in place, waiting for them. That night I searched the house for a Bible, looking for the verse that had the words, "Let not your heart be troubled." My mother said this to me, so many times, but her version was "Let not your heart be troubled, Bunky." And so I endeavored to find this passage with the idea of reading it (without the Bunky part) at the graveside the next morning. I wanted someone who knew my mother to say something at her burial, not just the pastor in her hometown who she didn't actually know. I could do this. I can be the child who does this for her mother.

Precipice

I found the Bible on the bookshelf in the TV room, the inside inscription with my brother's name. It would, of course, be his Bible that I would find. Late that night, he arrived. We set out the next morning from the funeral home, driving in a tiny caravan to the cemetery where I sat on a folding chair next to my father holding the Bible with the passage marked. I repeated in my head "Let not your heart be troubled. Let not your heart be troubled. Let not your heart be troubled." I held on to the Bible with both hands. At the end of the service, I stood up, walked past the headstones of my grandparents across the grassy hill and handed the Bible to my brother. "This is yours, John."

THE CURSE AND THE BLESSING
DAWN HOBBIE STICKLEN

I can't believe it's been 15 years.

I close my eyes and instantly I'm transported back to that front lawn, my face buried in my hands. I try to scream, but my desperate yells sound more like a squeaky whisper than the loud bellow I intend, "Call 911! Call 911!" Can anyone hear me? Where is everyone? My legs, usually so strong and steady, suddenly forsake me, buckling below my torso, sending me crashing to the ground. I am utterly helpless, completely alone.

I hear the sirens morph from a faint whistle to a steady, insistent blare as they draw near. Behind me, in the back yard, my brother-in-law hauls my son's lifeless body from the swimming pool. When the paramedics arrive, they immediately race around back in order to relieve my brother-in-law from his futile CPR attempts.

After they load my baby's limp body into the ambulance, I let them carry me to the car and we follow behind to the hospital.

"We're going to have to do an MRI to see if there is any brain activity." Lacking any desire to speak, I merely stare up at the doctor's face as she advises me of her assessment.

In the waiting room the doctor demands responses to questions I cannot possibly answer: "How long was he in the water? Where did you find him? Did you perform CPR?" In her eyes I see the condemnation she doesn't speak. To her, I am just another irresponsible, daft, young mother. She has no way of knowing the truth – that I am overly diligent about his safety. She doesn't know that we removed our patio furniture at home to keep him from climbing on it and falling off the two-story deck. She doesn't know that we won't travel without our children. She doesn't know my apprehension about staying at the house with the pool in the backyard. To her, I am negligent, an unfit mother.

I stand beside his bed, holding his limp little hand in mine. I pray, "God, please, just let him live. I don't care how you do it. Please, please don't take him from us."

But they are just empty thoughts – words which, despite my better judgment, I can't help muttering over and over again in my anguish and despair.

I read to him endlessly. I cry, turning my face away so he doesn't see me. I have no idea why I do this, though, because he is still unresponsive.

How many days pass? Two? Three? Four? Finally I

decide to shower, a useless attempt to wash away the unbearable agony, and am only in long enough to soap up when I hear the shouts, "Get out of there, now! They need you!"

His heart has stopped beating.

Slowly, deliberately, they remove the tubes from his body, and place him in my arms. I hold him, begging him to please open his eyes. I just want to see his smile one more time. How could this happen?

My God, my God! Why hast thou forsaken me?

My life is over.

Here I sit, thinking about how everything went wrong, why I couldn't stop the avalanche once it began its descent down the mountain. I wonder how my life would have been different — and it most certainly would be different — if I had only gone to check on him five minutes earlier.

Would I change it, if I could?

Learning to live through — and with — grief is one of the most difficult things I have ever done. Somewhere along the line I read that grief has many different stages. I wish I could tell you I remember experiencing them all, but I can't. My grief was more like moving through a very heavy, zero-visibility fog. Sometimes the fog would lift, teasing me with a glimpse of daylight. During these times I would allow myself the luxury of enjoying time with my daughter or my husband or my friends. Then, suddenly and without warning, the fog would return, clouding my memories for what seemed to be all eternity.

Slowly, little by little, the fog began to lift

permanently. We began to talk about the future as if it might really exist for us. Eighteen months after my son died, I reached a turning point: if I must be here, then I no longer wanted to merely exist. I wanted to *live*.

Living, for my husband and me, meant consciously putting forth the effort required to ensure the well-being of our daughter as well as ourselves. Living also meant procrastination was no longer a luxury we could afford. For almost five years I had listened in earnest to stories of families who came together through adoption. I began dreaming about foreign adoption and what it might be like to be an "adoptive mom." After my son's death, "now" became the time to do everything I had put off in earlier years.

Gradually we returned to life. We opened our hearts to the unexpected. We adopted our first son and during the adoption process discovered we were pregnant with our second daughter. Christmas two years later found us back in Russia for our second adoption. Our oldest daughter once again had siblings in her life, and we accepted the responsibilities and joys of being parents all over again.

Sometimes I think the hardest part is this: missing someone so desperately and trying to maintain some connection to the past while, at the same time, overflowing with gratitude for the joy of knowing the reality of today. It's incredibly unfair.

To ask the Fates to spare me from this pain would also mean to relinquish the pleasure of having all the other emotions I continue to experience in my new reality. It would diminish the ability to really, truly feel – not just raw, debilitating, pain, but also intense, unconditional love. Fear is also a part of the emotional mixture, but fear always accompanies love.

Normal days – the ones that pass by unmarked by a significant milestone — I don't think about it. I immerse myself completely in life, because that is the one conscious decision I was allowed during the Experience. If I have to stay here, then I will be an active participant. This, for me, is both the curse and the blessing.

But today it's been 15 years, and I must think about it. Whether it's fair or not, it has become part of my life.

CHRISTMAS BALLS
ANGIE KINGHORN

When my father was diagnosed with prostate cancer at the tender age of 51, he decided to keep it a secret. I thought he was crazy. I didn't understand.

When my husband was diagnosed with testicular cancer, only a year after my father died, he decided to tell people about it. Even though they'd learn he'd had a testicle removed.

In this culture where everything's about balls — having the balls to do something, taking the world by the balls, having a pair of big brass ones — he had no problem with anyone knowing he had only one.

Neither did I. I was proud of his decision, of his openness. Because of his decision to share his experience, several family members and friends learned a lot about testicular cancer, and a few even went to the doctor to be checked.

But it wasn't exactly perfect. During the next year's Christmas season, we went to a party.

"So what do Mark and the Carolina Panthers have in common?" the voice roared from the giant flatscreen. "They both play with only one ball!"

Our hostess had bottled Christmas and poured it liberally over her house. The smell of evergreen and spiced cider wafted through the warm, open-beamed space. Fraser fir branches and red votives topped every surface, and an astonishing stack of Christmas cards sprinkled the coffee table for our perusal.

This is not happening. This is not happening. This is NOT what I meant when I said I wanted to spread awareness about testicular cancer. Holy shit, what do we *do now?*

My cheeks already flushed from wine, the laughter of our friends harsh in my ears, I did the only thing I could think to do.

I gave my husband a high five.

His face is blurred out of that memory. Was he laughing? Shocked? Hurt? Embarrassed that his wife was celebrating his missing testicle as a punchline?

Punchline. Rolling the word around my head, I realized it did feel like a punch to the gut.

Earlier that day, we'd debated whether to go to the party. It's held every year among a small subset of our friends, and a roast has become traditional. I'm opposed to roasts on principle. There's a fine line between being roasted and burned, and even the professionals screw it up.

My introduction to roasts was in college, where my

sorority held an annual "Senior Burns" roast. After my first year I skipped the experience. And I wish I could un-hear the things I heard at the first one, because to this day when I see Facebook pictures of certain girls, the things that come to mind are stories of sexual escapades and virginity lost on the house sofa, or the places they vomited, or oh, yeah, that's the girl that got drunk and peed in the closet. And that? Is not the sum of those women.

Any more than the lack of a testicle is the sum of any man.

Later, I thought of my hand raised in that high five and wondered if I should have given a different hand gesture. One with four less fingers. Ended the party right there, said, "Screw you all. This is not up for laughs."

But I didn't.

Because I wanted my husband to be able to save face. You're not any less of a man with one testicle, no matter what people might think. Sex works, and works the same way. And I high fived him to say, in front of everyone, that he was a man even without that excess testicle, that words couldn't hurt us.

But those words were agonizing, and that night I discovered that the same mama bear instincts that get triggered when my children are in danger also come out when my husband is threatened. And watch out, because mama bear has serious claws.

This cancer? Not up for roasting. Not in my world. Not in the world where surgeons had to remove a body part from my husband less than 24 hours after we discovered the tumor because it was *that urgent*. Not in a world where we were considered lucky because the tumor grew so quickly that it outgrew its blood supply and became necrotic, causing pain so severe he couldn't ignore it. It was terrifying; major surgery and six weeks of daily radiation, watching his face get grayer each day.

Post-roast, I fled to the bathroom, ran cold water over my wrists and thought about what I should have said. If one of the women in our group had breast cancer and a mastectomy, would they make fun of her missing breast? What about all the couples among us that struggled with infertility? Was that up for grabs as a roast subject, too?

When I emerged, most of the men were swaying where they stood, clapping each other on the back and slurring "Merry Chrishmas!" The women were gathered in knots of wine-soaked too-loud laughter. It was that nightmare where you're screaming your head off in a crowded room and nobody can hear it. Talking with anyone at that point would have been as effective as trying to commune with spirits over an Ouija board.

My husband seemed fine, laughing and drinking a beer. But those words had scraped across *my* skin like barbed wire, opening old wounds and salting them.

My father always told me to grow a thicker skin. To let things roll off me like water off a duck's back. As if it could be so easy.

I never understood why my father didn't want to tell anyone about his prostate cancer. For the 12 years he suffered, I was baffled by his silence.

I fought his edict tooth and nail. I needed to talk to my friends. I was terrified I would lose him. He needed to talk about it, and I begged him to go to therapy, begged until one day, standing in the front yard, he told me that if I ever brought it up again to get out of the house and not come back. It was vitally important to him that nobody know, that this cancer be a secret, even as he got sicker, even as he cut back on work hours and then shut down his practice. Even as he began to have severe medication-induced hot flashes and began to turn down invitations to almost all social engagements. Even as he stopped playing golf. Even as his friends stopped calling.

Standing at that party, seething in the aftermath of the roast, I wondered if this was his fear. Public humiliation. Friends wondering what his cancer had done to him in the bedroom.

Two years too late, I got it. I got it, alone in a room full of holiday cheer. I got it, and finally, two years too late, I respected his choice.

The roast still burned, though. Just as the pain of a burn lingers, it was there, at the edges of my conscious mind, for months.

Be the duck, I told myself. *Let it roll off your back. Be the duck. Quack if you have to, but be the damn duck.*

I tried, for a week after the party.

But here's the thing. As an adult, I've finally figured out what I am. I'm not a duck. I'm a bear.

Which is why I found myself on the phone with the friend who coordinated the roast, spelling out in detail exactly how not funny this cancer experience was.

"I'm so, so, sorry," he said. "I honestly had no idea."

"You need to understand; it didn't upset Mark," I said, "but it devastated me. It was the most terrifying time of my life. My father had just died and Mark was diagnosed with cancer only a year later. All the men in my family except Mark have died — I still have nightmares that he's dead! I don't go anywhere without Xanax because I don't know when I'll have a panic attack."

After a lot of talking, we resolved it, and this guy and his wife remain some of our closest friends. And perhaps I should thank him, because really, if nothing else, the whole roast did answer a question that has plagued me since 1997. Why did my father want to keep his cancer a secret?

I think I know now. Dad's decision is less of a mystery. But I'm even more proud of my husband for making the opposite decision.

Sharing your cancer? That takes balls.

MORE THAN A BLANKET
VICTORIA KIRICHOK

I pull the Batman sheets off my son's bed, careful not to include any of his stuffed animals in the laundry. The top bunk is cluttered with creatures from traditional brown teddy bears to a fantastic green dragon with shiny wings. Amid the plush menagerie is a baby's blanket. Years ago it was powder blue with soft shiny trim. Now it's browning with age and gets a little crusty between washings. The satin binding has been repaired many times. My uneven zig zag stitches create small lumps here and there.

When Owen was small he didn't want a pacifier and he didn't suck his thumb. He never even took a bottle. For the first few months of his life I was his pacifier. Seeing me grow weary of that role, my mother said, "He needs a blanket with a satin edge."

I couldn't imagine why that would help. Why would

one particular kind of blanket work when every brand of pacifiers on the market had failed? But I was willing to try anything at that point. "We have one," I told her. "There was a blue blanket like that in the gift basket they gave me at the office."

She hunted around the nursery and found the blanket. She presented it to Owen as if it was the Holy Grail. He immediately took it in his arms with a smile and rubbed his face against the satin binding. From that moment, the only time he was without that blanket was when I pried it from his hands so I could wash it. My mother was right. He needed a blanket with a satin edge. Apparently, when you've raised four children of your own and had ten grandchildren and sixteen nieces and nephews, you learn a thing or two about babies.

Owen squeezed and chewed the blanket as he fell asleep for years. He wore it as a superhero cape. It cured carsickness, nightmares, hurt feelings and insomnia. Owen didn't use the pronoun "it" when talking about Mankie, he would say "he" or "she". I forgot to pack Mankie on one vacation — Owen barely slept for five days.

A children's librarian once heard me call Owen by name and suggested we check out the book *Owen* by Kevin Henkes. In the book, Owen is a mouse who has a favorite yellow blanket named Fuzzy who goes everywhere with him. A nosy neighbor named Mrs. Tweezers convinces Owen's parents that he's too old for Fuzzy. They try dipping the edge of Fuzzy in vinegar and being stern but Owen isn't ready to surrender Fuzzy.

As I read the book to my Owen I could feel him getting tense and holding Mankie closer and closer. At the end of the book, Owen and his mother come up with the idea of cutting up Fuzzy and making handkerchiefs out of it. I should have read Owen *The Shining* by Stephen King. He would have been less disturbed.

We created some rules about Mankie as Owen got a little older, but I never tried to make him give it up. Mankie lives in the bedroom and can only come out to be washed or taken on long car rides. Mankie is threadbare and stained and smelly, but sometimes it comforts my growing boy. I was given many baby blankets when I was pregnant — colorful quilts and hand knitted afghans and countless flannel swaddling blankets. And there was a simple blue blanket with satin trim. I didn't know a blanket could do more than keep a child warm.

HOSPITALITY LOST AND FOUND
DIANE TARANTINI

I can't remember if I trembled when they asked. I'm pretty sure I did. The question came in an e-mail but would've been cooler if it had arrived via telegraph.

Coming to your town for five days STOP
Can we stay with you STOP
Or at least share one good Italian meal

I cupped my hand under my mouth to catch the excuses as they flowed. Mostly buts. But I think Big Girl (our oldest daughter and their missionary nanny for three months) will be at college by then. But we have a softball tournament that weekend. But we don't really have enough room. Folks will have to sleep on the sofa. And the floor. But I'm intimidated. Because the wife mommy is a food blogger. And I'm freaked. What if she's also a white-gloved dust inspector? The house hasn't been cleaned, really spiffed up, in so long.

And yet, how could I say no? Big Girl had lived with them for a quarter of a year. In a compact casa in Honduras. They shared their every meal, their children, and their vision with her. I couldn't say no. But I wanted to. Was ashamed that I considered it.

I tried to say, "*Mi casa es tu casa*," but I couldn't get my Irish, German, English, French lips around the words, much less the concept. The only way I can achieve a really good Spanish accent is to mimic the Verizon recording, "Para Espanol, marque el dos."

Where did they go — my gift of hospitality, my spirit of generosity? I grew up. Little Me ("Wanna figure out how many licks it takes to get to the center of a Tootsie Roll Lollipop? Here, you go first.") was cannibalized by Grown-up Me ("Me, my, mine. That's all I have time for.").

Honk! Honk! Honk!

Big Girl clambered down the stairs. "They're here."

I heard jubilation in her voice. I hope she sounds like that when she speaks of us — her real family.

I peeked out the foyer window as she sprinted toward the street. My eyes bugged as all five of them tumbled out of a dusty old van.

The wife mommy's hair was like whipped cream with one drop of yellow food coloring. But her eyes weren't blue. With hair that Swedish looking I would've thought they'd be glacier, no, fjord, blue. If I took a glass prep bowl and filled it with good quality Italian olive oil and whisked in vanilla? That would be the color of her eyes. She was tinier than me, with an elegant slice to her deltoids.

Now he, the husband daddy, was a Mr. America leprechaun. His dark hair was pushed up into a singular wave. From inside the house I could feel his just-bonked-a-tuning-fork-on-a-brick energy undulate toward me. I possess that vitality too but somehow while they were here, I felt subdued. Calm not jangly, hot chocolate instead of espresso.

All three offspring had blue, surprised eyes and banana-colored hair. Baby boy buried his face in wife mommy's neck. The two toddler girls catapulted into Big Girl's embrace.

"We missed you! Tell us a story!"

Unnoticed, I pressed my nose against the screen door. Waited to face plant into the invisible ice-cube structure I was sure would exist between us. I know, I thought. I'll fetch my crème brulee torch. But I didn't need to. When they climbed onto the front porch, I didn't even get goosebumps.

Only I knew what I'd done. And it was bad. Sort of. Over the past few weeks I'd crafted a plan, a schedule, to keep them busy. Away from our house. Because really, how could ten people in a hundred-year-old house for five days be good? I arranged sights for them to see. Over in the next county. Swim, tour, cook out, repeat.

With other families. In their homes. Go, go, go. Vroom, vroom, vroom. Then they'd pass out every night by nine, right?

And then came the day they didn't want to go anywhere. They just wanted to be. Here.

"We like your house best," they said.

My eyebrows lifted beneath my bangs. "Really?"

"Really."

"It's like a super cool, artsy bed and breakfast."

My shoulders fell. My face tilted. The corners of my mouth lifted.

"Nap time," the husband daddy proclaimed. He stood — the boy baby in his arms, a toddler girl on either side. They headed for the stairs.

And then we were alone. The wife mommy and me. I checked my watch. Tied my shoes. What do we do now, I thought.

"Wanna cook some stuff?" I said.

She grinned and followed me into the kitchen.

Over at the counter, I sliced strawberries into thin, red halos. Seated at the table, wife mommy showered them in balsamic vinegar. Sprinkled them with raw sugar. We ate. And smiled.

I peeled and chopped roasted golden beets. Vinaigretted them. Rained down toasted pecans and tiny diced feta.

"Add that to the list," wife mommy said, "of recipes you have to send me."

I handed her the menu from our Italian Feast Night. "Mark all the things you want recipes for."

She circled almost every item then turned her attention to the shitake mushrooms from the farmers market. She sautéed them in golden green olive oil with heaps of garlic minced by me. She flicked in a speck of Silafunghi, my favorite Italian hot pepper concoction. Stirred. Lifted the wooden spoon to her lips.

"Wait!" I said. I pressed the spoon back into the sauté pan. "Don't taste it yet." I held up my pointer finger. "I have to do one thing."

I darted outside to my herb garden. Used my fingernails to nip off the largest sage leaves I could find. Brushed the soil flecks away. Grinned as I remembered my mom's philosophy — You gotta eat a peck of dirt before you die.

I returned to the kitchen. Floated the silvery leaves in hot oil. Flipped them when they became see-through. Used my grandmother's thongs to hold them up to the light.

"See? Don't they look like stained glass? Or an old Coke bottle? Now put some of the mushrooms on your fork. Top them with a crispy sage leaf. Taste it now."

I held my breath and watched. Her tongue worked. Her eyelids fluttered. She held up both her thumbs. I laughed.

As she prepped another bite to eat, I whispered. So she wouldn't hear me. Turned away. So she couldn't see my mouth move.

"I wish you lived here," I said to the refrigerator door. "Then we could be friends. We could eat like this over and over. Not one Sunday afternoon and never again."

The next day, Big Girl and I waved as their van drove away. The morning sun glinted off my daughter's tear tracks. I didn't cry. I was too busy working on my accent. In my head. Trying to get it just right. In case they circled the block and stopped in front of our house for one more Big Girl hug or kiss. But they didn't come back. If they had, I would've run down the steps to the street. Pecked on the husband daddy's window till he rolled it down.

"Just so you know, *mi casa es tu casa*."

Fiction

STICKY'S CAKE
SHELTON KEYS DUNNING

"Sticky, no one is going to know what this is all for," Sellamina protested calmly.

Sticky-Tagger shrugged at his sister and placed a flowered swag over the knot in their tree. He put flowers everywhere he could think of. Daffodillys draped off of every branch and toadstool. Button roses were stuffed into every crevice. Petals lined the forest floor already weighed down by a thick layer of pine needles. "Are we having cold-wings already?" he asked her.

"No, I said I'd be here, and I am, but no one will understand any of it," she pouted then stretched out her arms and basked in a ray of sunshine. The golden light caused her copper skin to shimmer, mesmerizing Sticky momentarily. He couldn't help but copy her movement, as if her mirrored reflection in the still water of a pond. They were a unique pair. Not only did they hatch from the same cocoon, a rarity in itself, they both bore the same sun-kissed hues in nearly identical patterns. "Your obsession with humans will be the end of you someday," she warned him. 'You've had too many close calls. It's a wonder the Seeress hasn't kicked us out of the clan."

"The Seeress is as fascinated as I am," he said in self-defense. "She says the more we know about them, the safer we'll be."

"I know, but I still wish she didn't indulge you as much. You take way too many unnecessary risks."

"Do you think we need more flowers?" he asked her while investigating a small, flower-free patch of forest floor.

She shot him the look that withers butterflies, "We've pulled up every stinking daisy, marsigoldy, and squishy-blossom in the whole acre for this little stunt of yours. What could we possibly need with more?"

Sticky frowned, hurt, and fidgeted with the ends of his wings. He wanted the bright paper streamers he remembered seeing the humans use. The reds, yellows, and blues festooned off of the eaves of houses and dangled daintily over the streets on stretched wires. The flowers, while a nice substitute, just weren't the same. His sister was forcing him to make do.

Pocker and Lily-Fathri arrived then, their scaly, moss like wings fluttering noiselessly as they descended to perch on the northern-most toadstool. "Sticky-Tagger," Pocker announced excitedly. "Lily and I brought our thimbles!"

Lily displayed equal excitement, quivering as if

unable to sit still. "We even polished them with acorn oil so they'd gleam."

Sellamina shook her head and groaned. "Do you know why?" she asked them, a hint of annoyance lurking in her voice.

They both looked confused. "Sticky asked us to?" Lily replied, timidly. "Ooh, you made a flower fort!"

"He made more than one flower fort," Topple croaked. He balanced precariously on an overhead branch cycling through failed attempts of an appropriate chameleon pattern to his surroundings. "I have to point out that flower forts won't protect us from the balinogs."

Sticky shivered at the thought, but not because the amphibians were a pixie's most nightmarish predators. Topple had an overdeveloped sense of paranoia, often spending all his flight energies on practicing camouflage in defense against creatures who were colorblind. "Balinogs are hibernating, Topple. It's still too cold for them."

Topple, unconvinced, attempted a new hue of brown. "We'll see."

The friends exchanged worried glances at Topple's expense. If the other guests believed there was a possibility of attracting balinogs, they wouldn't come. Sticky pleaded with them silently to do something. Pocker made a show of sniffing at the air, "Yes, just relax Topple, I don't smell balinogs anywhere. But I do smell something else." His ears perked forward, "Something gooey!"

"I forgot the cake!" Sticky announced. Rushing for

the knot, he ran up the bark and darted inside. Some salvaged scrap metal formed a solar-oven in the corner of their hollow under a shaft of light that perforated the trunk. He touched a finger to the baking cake, testing the firmness. His first cake ever was still a bit tacky to the touch. Frowning, he wondered if he had to wait another minute for the gooey to be less gooey. A reliable source told him that this is what humans made to celebrate the day, and he wanted everything to be perfect. Inhaling deeply, he savored the moment. The air smelled like warmed almond-honey-paste cake was supposed to, which he took as a good sign. Carefully, he pulled it from the oven and flew it gently out to a stone in the center of the flower forts.

More pixies from the Sundial clan had arrived during his absence, donning their thimbles like hats. *Word of the party must have spread,* he thought, not recognizing a few tawny-colored sprites in the midst of those assembled. Between the extravagant display of flowers and the striking contrasts in the pixies' plumage, swirls of colors made his patch of the woods extraordinary. Sticky thought he might explode from euphoria. His wings tingled and his flesh was consumed by goosiepimples. He shot a smile to Sellamina, who hid behind her wings from embarrassment. "Stupid human rituals," she muttered.

The crowd stared at him with hopeful faces. "We gather here today to celebrate a briftay," Sticky announced happily, once he was sure the cake was settled without shock. A collective sigh escaped the clan in response.

Sellamina corrected his pronunciation, "Birfday."

"Yea!" responded a chorus of pixies who broke out into spontaneous dancing, scattering flower petals to the breeze.

"Oh," Pocker said, his enthusiastic nod drifting gradually into a puzzled pause. "Sticky, what's a birfday?"

Lily replied excitedly, "Who cares what a berday is, there's cake!"

Topple, now white against a mushroom, groaned, "I'll bet that's what balinogs think when they see pixies."

"Don't be silly. Balinogs don't eat cake." Pocker stated, crossing his arms emphatically.

"I'll bet they do and I'll bet they think pixies taste better!" Topple insisted, pitch rising to form a panicked screech.

"Oh yeah, well I can see you!" Sticky snapped, beginning to doubt the wisdom behind his invite as pixies stopped dancing around them.

Topple frowned and spun about to chase his wings. "No you can't! Take it back!"

The joyous gathering was in danger of falling apart. The other pixies waited expectantly, eyes reflecting confusion as Topple went round and round in wasted effort to see the back of his wings. As Sellamina cast him another withering butterfly look, Sticky searched for a way to contain the growing concern.

"So," Lily said, eyeing the cake covetously and licking her lips, "What happens next?"

"Right! Thank you, Lily, for reminding me." Worried glances evaporated as Topple's endeavors went abandoned and attention was restored to Sticky. He cleared his throat and announced, "Next we all sing a little song and then — and this is the best part — we set the cake on fire and take turns blowing it out!"

SILENT TREATMENT
JULIE C. GARDNER

The bells here are louder than they need to be, as if they assume we might need waking. Maybe they have a point. I have been sitting at this desk for only five minutes and already my feet are numb. The teacher is pretty, in a non-threatening way. Her dress is loose and flowery; her blond hair clean, cut neatly at the chin. The scent of white-board marker stings my nose as she caps her pen and moves toward us.

"Kristy Alpert?" The teacher's words sail over the podium.

"Here," a shrill voice replies. I glance to my left at the bony girl whose dark curls spill onto her forehead. Her jaw twitches and I realize that Kristy has not changed.

"John Bartniki?"

"Yo," blurts a boy behind me and I picture J.B.: the

70

carrot-red head and freckles, the thin scar slicing across his brow. These are details I can conjure without turning around to confirm.

"Jane Davis?"

I raise a hand slowly, fingers splayed. The teacher scans the classroom, squinting in the fluorescent light. She acknowledges my signal with a nod, then looks down to continue calling roll.

So. It will not be Ms. Jones who tempts me to speak today.

I embarked on this silence at breakfast, my dad providing the first test. He was not a challenge. "Morning," he mumbled from behind the business section. When I did not respond, he simply fished for another spoonful of cornflakes.

My mom bustled into the kitchen, the belt of her tired bathrobe knotted thickly at the waist. She said, "Big day!" then brushed a dry kiss across the top of my head and grabbed a piece of toast that looked like it had been in the oven for a week. She scraped the charred bread with one edge of a knife (*tick tick tick*) then buttered the shredded remains with the other. She took a bite and chewed without sitting, dark crumbs clinging to her bottom lip.

And that was it.

By the time the bus lumbered to a stop across the street, Dad had folded his paper into a square, refilled his *World's Best Father!* mug with a flood of black coffee and disappeared into his office off the garage. Mom was matching socks in the laundry room. She called, "Don't forget your backpack!" as the front door groaned on its hinges and I stepped onto the porch.

I had thought the ride to school might present the biggest obstacle. I was wrong. Maybe the thirty-four other students were distracted by the stickiness of skin against green vinyl seats or disappointed about the end of summer vacation. Perhaps it was Maury the bus driver — perched high and glaring — who killed the mood. Whatever the reason, no one spoke as we rumbled toward Wilton High.

So here I sit — feet numb, mouth shut — in Ms. Jones' freshman English class waiting to see what is different. Clearly not the students. Our social groups have not shuffled since kindergarten; except, of course, for the Lauren Hindley Incident. She spent the summer before eighth grade in Europe and came back beautiful. I've never been to Europe so I look the same. Brown eyes, brown hair, brown life.

That is why I am silent today. Today, I am different.

Another deafening bell. Period one is over, then period two. I spend the early break rummaging in my locker, pretending to be occupied with the arranging of textbooks. Period three. Period four. Four teachers have nodded at my raised hand, slid course descriptions and homework sheets onto my desk. No one wants to hear from us today. I am no exception. Lunch is a line to acquire student IDs, our forms already completed, no questions asked or answered. Fifth period, sixth. The final bell echoes along corridors that fill quickly.

"Let's meet at the flag pole!" calls Lauren Hindley to someone who is not me.

I trudge past stucco buildings, count squares of cracked concrete on the path toward the parking lot. The morning's quiet rows now host pairs of friends debating first impressions of our campus. I sit across from the bus driver, his eyes fixed on a series of streets lined with two-story houses and maple trees. Maury does not ask what I thought of geometry or biology or the picture on my ID card. He does not notice the change in me.

I spend the afternoon in my room staring at a blank notebook. Each second on the desk clock brings me closer to my goal. Mom peeks in at 4:40, a grin on her face, amusement on her tongue.

"Look at you, overworked already! High school's a whole new ballgame, huh?" I do not correct her. The clock speaks (*tick tick tick*) and the shadows lengthen across my bed.

"Dinner's ready!" my mother calls at six o' clock. I climb down the stairs past a trail of school pictures framed on the wall: a missing tooth here, too-short bangs there. The kitchen is deserted but the smell of tomato lingers. I step into the dining room and see everything in a flash of my dad's camera: the overburdened pasta platter, the chocolate cake, my parents' eager smiles.

"Happy Birthday!" they shout, breaking into song. There are candles and balloons, icing to lick and polished silverware. Then – too soon – the tune is over and they are waiting for me. We are waiting for what comes next.

I look at my mother's puzzled face and feel myself slipping away. But even as I slide, I know what I am supposed to do. After all, we have been here before. So I take a deep breath, exhale sharply and blow the last candle out.

"Did you make a wish?" asks my mother, the ease returning to her cheeks.

"Yes," I say. Narrow threads of smoke curl toward the ceiling.

And just like that, I am fifteen. I am still Jane. And absolutely nothing has changed.

ESCAPE
SHELTON KEYS DUNNING

Everything baked in the afternoon sun as invisible waves of heat distorted her vision. Ivy, sick and dismayed, gripped her camera. Butchered corpses, animal and human, lay intermingled in the village square. The sweet, sticky smell of blood clung to the heavy equatorial air. She stood in the sea of death, fighting tears and the urge to vomit. Her finger twitched and the shutter fired as rapid as an automatic rifle. She was running out of daylight and on her last batteries, but it needed to be done. The world needed to know the evil she had witnessed here.

Broken familiar faces had met their demises with terror and pain. The spark of life was long departed from their dull eyes, their mouths trapped in the last words of their screams. Through the lens she spied Etsula, her little hand still gripping tightly to the cornhusk doll Ivy had given her only a week ago. "No," she whispered, heartsick. "Who slaughters children?"

"This is Tobago's handiwork," a deep voice rang out as a man emerged from the surrounding jungle. He sported camouflage fatigues, a pack on his back and a double-barrel shotgun slung across his shoulders. "You hurt, Lady?" he asked, his tone lacking the concern his words implied.

"No," she ventured hesitantly, unsure of his intentions. "I wasn't here when … when this …"

He nodded, slowly approaching. "I'm Mitch, I'm, well, a … liaison …working with the United States military. You Ivy Tanner, that reporter everyone's looking for?"

Her stomach lurched into her lungs. Was she the reason the whole village was massacred? Tobago knew who she was and was looking for her? Ivy dropped to her knees, unable to stand under the crushing weight of her guilt. "God," she uttered. "Forgive me."

"Look," he rushed the last few steps to fetch her up. "I don't mean to be an ass but we're too exposed. This area is infested with Tobago's goons."

She held the unseeing gaze of the sweet little girl not even old enough to understand the evil that brought an end to her simple world. "This was my first foreign assignment," she said, her voice broken. "My first and I br-brought doom to …"

The chopping sound of an approaching helicopter echoed in the distance. He grabbed her arm and dragged her to the undergrowth. "You didn't do this, the devil did," he growled. "Trust me later. Right now, we need to hustle to that landing pad."

Adrenaline surged through her veins, moving her legs when her heart couldn't bear to leave. She managed to run after him across the jungle floor. The helicopter was uncomfortably loud even muffled from the leafy ceiling. Mitch appeared to give it little pause, moving like a jaguar through the vegetation. She stumbled, a stick lacerating her leg, but she pressed onward as the distance between them grew rapidly.

Ivy tried to get her bearings when she lost sight of him completely. Her leg throbbed, distracting her concentration. She needed to rest. Crouching near a massive tree trunk, she wondered how sensible it was to hide when she had no idea where she was.

The helicopter eventually moved on, the percussive din dissipating rapidly. She sighed, happy to hear her own thoughts again. The chirp of her camera indicated exhausted batteries just as the sound of nearby gunfire echoed around her. Peering out behind her trunk, she spied Mitch in the middle of a standoff. Before she could react, someone grabbed her. She felt a blade's cold sting at her chin. Mitch froze instantly, boxed in by materializing guerillas.

Her camera bag was stripped from her shoulder and her captor threw her forward. "Las pilas están agotadas," he said.

She made eye-contact with Mitch, willing an apology to be silently communicated in the gesture. Her hair grabbed again, her head was pulled back, exposing her neck.

The blade slid across the base of her jawline. Ivy felt the hot, acidic breath of the guerrilla as he hissed in her ear, "I will give you the same deal I gave your pathetic villagers. Tell me what I want to know and I'll make your death clean, quick."

She closed her eyes. The sound of a whimpering puppy reached her before she realized it was her own throat making the wretched noise. If this was the end of her story, she wanted to face it bravely. She wanted to take someone with her when she plunged into the abyss. *Control your breathing.* Ivy summoned an ounce of courage from her soul and hoped it was enough. Steeling herself, she snapped, "Go to hell!"

She was struck by a fist the size of a mango. Reeling from the blow, she coughed, spitting blood from her mouth. Her leg refused to bend as she struggled to her knees. She was kicked back to the ground. Panting, she was a terrified puppy amidst a towering pack of angry wolves that would not rest until she was torn apart.

The guerrilla knelt on her injured leg, pinning her to the earth with a crushing weight. Ivy screamed as pain shocked every nerve of her body. Rough hands tore at her blouse. *No knife,* she thought, *he's using both hands unobstructed.* Seizing the opportunity, she clenched her fist and swung at his face with everything she had.

"Puta!" He punched her. Her vision blurred into a tunnel. She felt him punch her again.

A blitzkrieg of gunfire erupted around her and the weight of her assailant disappeared. Ivy couldn't move, afraid to betray her cognizance. Seconds turned into minutes before silence fell in the clearing. "Ivy!" Mitch was at her side, shaking her shoulder. "Tanner!"

"Yeah, I'm okay," she voiced, her throat raw despite the humidity. She stood awkwardly, moving slowly in comparison to her savior, who already moved on to loot his victims. Dead guerrillas were scattered across the clearing like discarded newspapers. Mitch threw a blood-stained shirt her way, which she donned numbly. "How did you …?" she breathed.

"Later," he answered. He investigated her camera. "Damn, it's busted. Here's the SD card."

"Thanks," she said, securing it in her pocket.

"Now let's get you to that chopper."

"Your shoulder," she said. Blood seeped in long rivers down his left-side from an obvious gunshot wound.

"My shoulder isn't important," he cut her off. "Right now, your pictures are the only hardcore evidence we've got against Tobago. I want to bring him down, don't you?"

She abandoned her protest. "I can't move very fast."

"We'll make it," he assured her, "as long as we start moving now."

"Do you think we'll encounter any more of them?" she asked, limping after him.

He paused briefly, his expression hard to read. "We'll make it," he repeated firmly.

They navigated through the jungle vines and ferns as quickly as her leg allowed. The remaining hike only served to provide time to think, not the promise of escape from trauma that she hoped for. Images of the villagers haunted her thoughts at each turn, disrupted only by fresh memory of her would-be rapist. She clutched at her procured chemise and probed gently at her swelling face. Her assailant, even dead, had left his mark on her.

They reached the edge of the clearing where freedom perched, protected by a dozen soldiers. Mitch stopped her to give his final instructions. "We'll be exposed again," he stated. "Nothing we can't handle, right?"

She nodded.

"Don't worry about me," he continued before she could protest. "I've worked with this crew before. Pilot's name is Birkhoff. He'll get you home. Now, no matter what happens, with or without me, you get to that chopper."

She didn't have time to think. He pushed her into the clearing and the helicopter blades started spinning. Ivy forced her legs to move, enduring the pain until her adrenaline engaged. The crew began to take and return fire and at one point, Mitch dropped from her peripheral vision. A soldier grabbed her before she could turn to search for him.

The crew took defensive positions around her and simultaneously helped her into the helicopter. A headset was slapped on her as she was strapped into a seat. She watched the open door for Mitch as she heard someone shout "Go! Go! Go!"

"Wait! Where's Mitch?" she cried. The faces around

her were grim and unresponsive. "No, we're not leaving him behind. He took a bullet for me!"

"So did three of my men," someone snapped. "Our orders are clear, Miss Tanner. We stick to the mission."

Tears leaked from her eyes, stinging her freshly bruised face. Outside, the azure sky shattered into shards of reds and oranges as she thought of the SD card in her pocket. She wasn't a warrior, or a hero, but she could write their story. The world will know of the brave, the truth. She owed the dead that much at least. And someday, someday very soon she promised herself, she was coming back for Mitch.

ABANDON
AMYBETH INVERNESS

It hurt far more than she expected. As a phlebotomist, Jude was used to needles. But the thousand tiny pricks never stopped. When she drew blood from a patient, she was able to comfort them with the promise that it would only pinch for a moment, and then it would be all over. The heavily inked and pierced young man she was paying to permanently mark her skin seemed more interested in flirting with her best friend than comforting her through the pain.

Renee had been the one to talk her into it in the first place. She had also been the one who chose the handsome young artists whose hands were currently fondling her breasts.

Perhaps "fondling" wasn't the best choice of word ... The initial planning stage had provided far more titillation than the actual procedure did. It just hurt far too much to be considered pleasurable. Renee had described the adrenaline rush she got with her first tattoo, but Jude experienced no such thing.

"Yeah, those are real nice ..." Herve had said after she unbuttoned her blouse. "I can definitely work with these." Jude had blushed from nose to toes at his words, but he just laughed. It wasn't a mean laugh; he went on to joke with her, putting her at ease and listening to what she wanted to do.

Renee had been with her through every session, just as she'd been by her side for all the appointments before. The ones that didn't work, and only made her sick to her stomach.

Jude used the hand mirror to take a better look at what Herve was currently working on. The large script R had come a little too close to her areola for comfort, but she was grateful for the sensation even though it was a negative one. Any sensation was better than none, and it had been a long time since any man had paid the slightest attention to her breasts. The smaller script E was done, and Herve wiped it clean before moving on to the next letter.

That night she sat alone in her apartment, most of the lights off so she could look out over the city. It sparkled and throbbed. It lived.

She was jealous.

For the third time in as many hours, Jude went to the bathroom and turned on the overly-bright make-up lights around the mirror. She opened her robe and examined the tattoo's progress. Her fingers delicately manipulated the tender flesh. The design was mostly on the top, where it could be seen by anyone who cared to notice if she dared to wear a low-cut blouse.

She added that to her to-do list: buy a low-cut blouse.

With the fingers of her left hand she covered her right nipple and gently lifted. The underside of her breast wasn't exactly pretty, but it was a canvas that could be used. She decided to have Herve add *jealousy* to the unused area.

She was running out of time. Normally, a tattoo artist would let the skin heal in between sessions, but Herve understood her urgency and made room in his schedule to accommodate her.

The morning before her final appointment, Renee called to apologize that she couldn't come. Her youngest was sick, and her husband had an out of town meeting he couldn't reschedule. Jude reassured her friend that it was all right; she was a big girl and could go to her appointment all by herself. She promised to come over after her session and show Renee the finished product.

"Hey, Jude!" Herve joked as he did every time he saw her. She was used to the old joke, being a Beatles fan herself. She didn't mind, just as long as he didn't start singing. "No Renee today?"

"No. She has to stay home with a sick kid." She wanted to say more. She wanted to banter with him like Renee did, to flirt shamelessly with the all-too-young man who was intimately familiar with her breasts. Words failed her. She just smiled her best "everything's all right" smile and followed him into a private room.

Jude managed to make a few appropriate responses to Herve's attempts at conversation, but soon after he started inking he gave up trying to engage her and just concentrated on touching up the details in his artwork. She closed her eyes, feeling guilty that she couldn't have a normal conversation with him, even after all the time they'd spent together.

The oscillating needles pricked her skin with the pain she'd come to love. Pain might be unpleasant, but at least it was a sensation. Better than the absence of sensation. Her mind wandered, indulging in a fantasy that the hunky young artist would gaze upon his work and declare it perfect ... and the touch of the needles would be replaced with the touch of his lips ... and then he would ravish her right there on the table, making her feel like a woman again.

A sigh escaped her lips. "You doing all right, Jude?" Herve asked. It didn't sound sexy at all. It sounded ... professional. As it should.

"Oh, I'm fine. Just ... you know."

Herve nodded and bent to his work again. Jude wanted to cry. She missed Renee. She needed her friend to be there, to pretend that everything was all right until Jude actually started to believe it. By the time Herve was done she was wound up so tight it hurt. On top of that, she was nauseated again, and weak. Yet she put on a brave face, praised Herve's work, tipped him well and made sure to tell his boss how happy she was with his work.

It was still red and a little swollen after a week, but

two weeks later she wore a scandalously low-cut little black dress as she and Renee attended the symphony. She enjoyed all the looks she got; the appraising ones from the men as well as the disapproving ones from their wives. She needed to feel sexy, just one last time.

Three weeks after the art was complete, Jude's mother came to stay. She even managed to smile throughout Jude's private photo shoot, although she didn't join in the tearful giggling Renee instigated. The images, permanently recorded on her skin, were transferred to the digital media from whence Jude could share her pain with the world ...

Or keep it private.

The doctors and nurses admired Herve's work, although some tsk-tsk'd about the idea of permanently scarring one's body while others tsk-tsk'd about what a shame it was to waste all that work.

By the end of the day, Herve's work was gone. Cut, destroyed, and sealed in some container labeled medical waste. Abandoned.

When the bandages came off and she went back to her apartment, she was glad to have her mother there. Reduced again to a flat-chested adolescent, haunted by unfamiliar and uncontrollable hormones. Late at night, when her mother was asleep, she went into the bathroom and turned on the over-bright lights again. She raised her arms and entwined her fingers behind her head, closed her eyes and imagined her breasts the way they had been. Glorious. Beautiful. Soft, round symbols of femininity.

She saw the words that Herve had scripted on the temporary flesh. Jealousy. Regret. Past mistakes. Worry. Pain.

All were abandoned.

THE SECOND
ANGIE KINGHORN

The letter was in the kitchen, sitting on the otherwise pristine countertop. No envelope, just her folded stationery next to an empty wine bottle.

Michael opened the creamy paper and saw that it was stained with scattered red spots, as if Virginia had shed tears of Pinot. The handwriting was clearly hers, but the words ran off the page in a tilt, and if the letter could speak, he knew the words would be slurred. He'd noticed the vodka bottles were draining more rapidly than usual, but how much *had* she been drinking lately? He tried to think about the past week but realized he hadn't seen her enough to know.

His footsteps echoed off the hardwoods and into the darkened hallways. Without the boys at home, the house was cavernous, looming. Virginia would already be in bed.

He usually worked late, and Virginia coped by taking evening appointments, saying she didn't like to be at home by herself until he managed to make it back from the office. Checking his watch, he realized it was 11:00. He couldn't blame her. This was too late.

Michael poured himself three fingers of bourbon, then settled into his leather armchair. There were a lot of notes lately, life memos left on the kitchen counter; their marriage reduced to inconsequential Post-its.

"Oh, damn," he sighed. "The dog." He let the Cavalier King Charles spaniel out of his crate into the back yard, leaving the French doors open to let the crisp air in. Once more, he sat down with Virginia's letter.

"Dear Michael,

I know you think what I do is quaint, a hobby more than a job, but you know, I hear a lot of fascinating things. People tell me their secrets.

Why don't you try and guess some? No, you probably don't have time. But try anyway. We haven't played a game together in a long time.

Your golf buddy, Nick, is gay. No, his wife doesn't know. True? False?

Your mother's ashes – I knocked them off the mantel last year and Marcella vacuumed them up. That urn is full of sand and ash from the cigarette container outside the main courthouse. True? False?

John's hunting accident last year? Not an accident. Eileen comes in to see me every week to try and deal with his suicide. And the fact that nobody knows. True or false, Michael?

You had an affair with your secretary 10 years ago. Brenda, I think it was. You thought I never knew, but she's the one who told me about all the late nights in the conference room. Never had an inkling I was your wife. True or false?"

"What the hell?" Michael stood up and strode down the hall. Virginia had gone off the deep end.

He turned on the lights in their darkened bedroom. "Virginia, wake up. We need to talk."

He turned to the bed, ready to shake his wife awake. The duvet was pristine. Virginia wasn't there.

"Virginia?" he called. She wasn't, as he'd found her before, asleep on the chaise lounge, or in one of the guest rooms, or one of the boys' rooms. *Where the hell was she?*

He dialed her cell phone as he walked back to the living room. He could hear it ringing in the kitchen. *Fabulous*, he thought. *Perfect night for her to disappear without her phone.*

He was trembling. How had she never said anything about Brenda? Was any of the other stuff true? She'd kept her name. People would have no reason to connect them.

He eyed the urn on the mantel, then finished off the bourbon and poured another before sitting to read more. The dog bounded in from the yard and barked. Michael patted the ottoman and he jumped up and settled in next to his legs.

"I know about your other secret, too." A giant drop of wine blurred the ink. "—stress turned out to be my

Thursday 8:00. At first all she told me was that she was seeing a married man. Mike. I didn't think anything of it. There's a thousand Mikes in the world, aren't there, *Michael?* Then she started to talk about his house. How he'd take her there when his wife wasn't home. How much she loved the kitchen. She said it was so cheery — yellow walls and yellow glass tile over granite."

Michael froze and turned his head to look toward the kitchen. Yellow walls, yellow glass tile. *But there had to be hundreds of kitchens like this.*

"A few weeks ago she told me about Mike's dog, this cute little spaniel. Though he had the weirdest name: Freud. Imagine that, Michael. *Freud.*"

"Freud?" Michael said, incredulous. The dog looked up and barked. "Oh, my God."

"And then last week, she tells me that she was going to end it, but Mike took her out to his pool house, which was just the most adorable thing ever, decorated in French yellow and blue toile, and told her he loved her and was going to leave his wife for her. Emily Post doesn't cover this, Michael, but I'm pretty sure this is NOT the way you tell your wife of thirty years you're leaving her for a younger woman.

After her session I found the bracelet on the couch where it fell off. I'm sure she'll want it back —" red wine smudge, "— velope on my desk in the kitchen.

–V."

Michael heard a key turn in the kitchen door and looked up, hoping to see Virginia. Instead, Chip burst in, nuzzling a giggling blonde on the neck.

Michael cleared his throat.

Chip closed the door and pinned the blonde up against the wall, now kissing her full on the mouth.

"Chip!"

"What?" Chip broke away from the blonde, who was most definitely *not* his wife, Caroline. "Dad? Sorry, I didn't realize anyone was here."

"Obviously." Virginia's letter was now clenched in Michael's fist. He walked over to the desk, and there it was. A lumpy envelope. He picked it up, blood thundering in his ears.

"Yeah, so, we'll just head out," Chip said, opening the door.

"No, you'll stay." Michael's voice was quiet, but hard. Chip shut the door.

Michael opened the envelope and a bracelet he'd never seen before tumbled out. He picked it up and studied it under the light. It held a single charm, and in the light, he read the inscription, "I promise. — MLC."

"Ohmigod! My bracelet!" shrieked the blonde. "I lost it last week. You found it here?"

Michael looked from the initials on the bracelet to the blonde, to his son, Michael.

"Chip, why don't you introduce me to your friend?"

Chip started. "Oh, that's ok, Dad, we were just leaving —"

"No, I insist."

Chip looked from his father to the girl to the bracelet in his father's clenched fist. He opened his mouth, but simply gaped like a fish.

Finally, the blonde broke the silence. "Hi, I'm Tiffany," she said. She stuck out her hand. Her nails were long, square, painted a sparkly pink. Michael didn't take it. He stared at Chip. Chip was studying his loafers. He wasn't wearing his wedding band.

"Um, anyway, can I have my bracelet back? I was so worried about it! Mike only gave it to me like, last week, and it's just until —"

"Tiffany!" Chip barked. "Just take it and go get a glass of wine, ok?"

She grabbed the bracelet from Michael's hand, her nails scraping his palm. "O-kaaay. I'll be down in the cellar. Let's have some more of that Bordeaux we tried last time? Maybe in the hot tub?"

"Tiff! Dammit, just go get something to drink."

Michael picked up the envelope, trying to piece things together through the bourbon. There was something else inside. Gently, he turned it upside down and one of Virginia's engraved cards fell to the counter.

"Dad, I can explain everything, just please don't say anything to Caroline ..." Chip's voice faded to a buzz as Michael turned the card over to see Virginia's careful script.

See how she likes the pool house now. She can have it for all I care.

"No!" Michael was already running, out the open French doors, across the wet grass. He could hear Chip yelling behind him. "Dad! What are you doing?"

Halfway across the lawn, he heard the gunshot.

He was too late.

HAND OF FATE
KELLY KOHLES

She almost fell into the simmering pan.

Twice.

Her eyes battled to stay open. After a night of hurling in the toilet between shots of vivid nightmares - then her daughter refusing to nap – it was all Elizabeth could do to remain standing.

You should check on Hannah. She's too quiet. The voice in her head always sounded like her mother-in-law, never satisfied.

But, Elizabeth argued back, *what if she's fine? She'll see me, throw a fit, and I'll burn dinner.*

Her feet remained rooted to the tile.

She swayed with the spoon, eyes closed, picturing a hot bubble bath: limbs buried in warmth, cucumbers on her eyes, and the soothing sounds of Enya as a soundtrack.

The breath was warm on her neck, lips tickling the fine hairs that escaped her harried ponytail. "Hey."

Elizabeth's hand jerked at his touch. The spoon in her hand flipped out of the pot, sending the tomato sauce across the granite countertop. Several drops landed on her hand, burning the skin. "Dammit, Mike! You scared the —"

"Daddeee!" Tiny bare feet slapped the tile and Elizabeth turned in time to see Hannah launch herself into Mike's arms. She flew into the air, screaming in delight as Mike spun her in a circle — all signs of the terrible three-year-old erased.

Elizabeth grabbed a towel, wiping the sauce from her skin, cleaning up her husband's mess while he flipped their daughter upside-down.

Hannah's laughter bubbled over them, and Elizabeth hid a smile as their routine unfolded.

"How's my favorite Pumpkin?"

"I not a punkin, Daddy." The giggles ceased as her daughter scolded her husband.

His jaw dropped in exaggerated surprise and lifted her up to face him. "You're not? Then what are you?"

"I'm a big girl." She pointed to her hair. "I made my hair pretty."

Elizabeth frowned and tossed the towel on the counter. "What do you mean you —" She froze as her daughter turned and faced her.

Giant hunks of precious midnight curls were absent on the right side — only one small strand remained. A small tuft stood straight up where she'd cut closer to the skin. The damage on the left side lacked the severity of the right, but no longer reached several inches past her shoulders. Only the very back remained unscathed.

"Hannah Jane Bauer, you are in big trouble!" She buried the screaming guilt — she knew Hannah had been too quiet. She reached for her daughter, watching as Hannah cringed away, clinging to her father.

"NO! I am big girl! I am not in trouble!"

"You know aren't supposed to take my scissors — they are dangerous!" Had she left them out last night, too exhausted to put them away?

"Liz, don't you think you're overreacting a bit? It's just hair." He cradled their daughter, as he always did. Hannah was his little angel.

Like Hannah was her demonic spawn. "You always make me the bad cop. I'm tired of it. She wants you? Fine. You discipline her!" She whirled away, tossing behind her shoulder, "Don't forget to take away Bobo." Time-outs never worked with Hannah — she never stayed put — so her stuffed tiger served time-out instead.

"Nooooooo! You don't take away Bobo! Bobo is mine!" Her piercing squeals echoed off walls, bulls-eying the headache Elizabeth had fought all day.

"Liz, is this really necessary?" He had to shout over Hannah's dramatic wails.

"For once can you act like my partner and support me instead of her?" Elizabeth heard the shrill tone creeping into her voice even as tears pricked behind her eyes. She took a deep breath. "Please?"

His brown eyes pierced hers and she had to look

away, refocusing on the sauce.

"Come on, Pumpkin. We have to put Bobo in time-out."

Hannah's screams became louder, then faded as Mike carried her to her room.

He never saw the silent tears pouring down Elizabeth's cheeks.

***

Thumpthumpthumpthump. Thumpthumpthumpthump. Over and over the pattern repeated — the percussion accompaniment to the music of Hannah's hoarse cries.

Elizabeth stared at her plate of pasta, moving it around but never taking a bite – nothing eaten today had stayed down and the last thing she wanted was to spend more time over the toilet.

"This is ridiculous, Liz. How long are we going to let this go on?"

She forced her gaze to his, noticing his plate was empty. "As long as it takes." Her daughter's stamina for tantrums grew each week. She knew giving in would only encourage the behavior. "More spaghetti?"

"Are you kidding? Is this what you do all day with her? Lock her in room and take away her favorite toys?"

She winced at his attack, hating the truth in his words even as her anger blossomed. "That's right. I'm a horrible mother. What do you know? You swoop home every night after a quiet day at work and she's smiles and sunshine. You don't see the hell I go through every day. I dare say the word "no" and she's on the floor screaming."

"I'm sure she isn't that bad."

She wanted to stab the derision out of his voice. With her fork. "Yes, Mike. She is. What she's doing now, is what she does all day. Every day."

Disbelief laced his face. "Not every day."

I will not use my fork as a weapon. "Sure, she's happy the few days you're actually home. You never tell her no and let her do whatever she wants. Grow a pair and tell her no and you'll see how fast she turns on you."

He shoved away from the table. "Grow a pair? What the hell, Liz?"

She closed her eyes, fighting for calm. "I need you to be her father, not her buddy. I need you to stop staring at me like I'm an evil stepmother. I had the shots of Clomid. I have the C-section scar. I am the one who has spent all day, every day with her since!" Tears spilled down her cheeks and she battled the full body sobs threatening to take over her body.

His features softened – he always hated seeing her cry. "I am her father." He moved toward her, slowly, as if she was a wild animal. "You're right, I hate denying Hannah anything, but isn't there a better way to punish her?"

Elizabeth opened her mouth, ready to argue, when she heard it: silence. "Mike, she stopped kicking." Her daughter began singing, and relief washed over her.

He stopped, cocking his head to listen. Surprise filled his face. "What do we do now?"

"Give her a few more minutes before inviting her to dinner."

"And then?"

"We wing it."

***

"There are night diapers in the bag and I packed her blankie. Oh, and extra clothes and some snacks, because she'll probably get hungry and —"

"Liz, I got it." Mike leaned forward, his unshaven face scraping her cheek as he brushed her lips. "We'll only be at my mom's overnight."

"I know, it's just —" in three years Elizabeth had never once spent a night away from Hannah "– maybe I should come too."

Mike rolled his eyes. "No way. You have a spa treatment booked."

Elizabeth bit her lip, wanting to undo her lie and confess about the doctor's visit planned. "Actually I —" she paused. *What if I jinx it? What if it's a hysterical pregnancy? Or the flu?* "I can't wait."

"Daddy, let's go!" Hannah bounded up behind them, the one-eyed Bobo in one arm and pulling her mini carry-on with the other.

"Not until I get a hug from my Hannah-girl." Elizabeth squatted, opening her arms.

Hannah gave her a look. "Mommy, my hands are too full."

Elizabeth swallowed. "A kiss then?"

Hannah beamed, coming closer and slobbering a big smack onto her lips as Elizabeth held her tight.

"I love you, Pumpkin."

"Mommy, I not a punkin."

Her smile met Mike's over her daughter's head.

"You're not? Then what are you?"

"I'm a big girl."

She watched them walk out the door, bags in tow, not knowing it would be the last time.

***

Elizabeth sat in front of the room, a sea strangers staring back at her, nerves dancing in her gut.

The cooing baby slung across her chest kicked her side, as if to chase the trepidation away.

She smiled down, lips trembling. "I can do this without crying, right?"

Happy gurgles answered.

Elizabeth took a deep breath. *For Mike and Hannah.*

"Our next speaker is sharing her story today. A very active member of MADD, please welcome Elizabeth Bauer."

Elizabeth rose, her legs shaky as she walked to the microphone. She traced the baby's toes with her finger, drawing strength from her little miracle.

"It was one year ago. My doctor confirmed I was seven weeks pregnant with Mikayla Hannah. My phone rang – I thought it was Mike returning my voice mail. Instead, my world shattered. My husband and three-year old daughter had been killed by a drunk driver."

SHALLOW GRAVE
JESSIE BISHOP POWELL

"Pick your glass," Miss Anna said. "There's three, all alike."

"Oh, no ma'am. We trust you," Trevor said quickly.

Miss Anna laughed. No music in her voice, but no needles, either. "No you don't. Nor would I in your shoes. Pick. But don't drink. Not yet."

"Did you really hex Mark for what he did to those cats?" asked Paul.

Miss Anna didn't laugh this time. Just shook her head.

"But you could have," Paul continued. It wasn't a question.

Miss Anna nodded.

The choice in beverages suddenly seemed very important indeed. Trevor closed his eyes and picked blind, then Paul did the same. Then, Miss Anna said,

"Now, which one of you saw it?"

And Trevor said, "Me," without hesitation. They weren't talking cats now.

"Shut up!" said Paul.

"I won't call the police. Be easy, child. We all know that stepfather of yours would have your mother dead before the fuzz finished digging up the grave, and he'd do it if she was at work and if work was a hundred miles away."

Paul sucked in a breath and looked at Trevor. Miss Anna had just repeated exactly what their stepfather, Randy had whispered to their mother when the two of them returned to the trailer from burying the yellow haired man.

"Me," Trevor repeated. "I saw. Do you need me to tell you?"

"No." The old woman shook her head. "Now's when we drink, by the way." They did, and Miss Anna continued, "I saw it, too, but I don't have any personal enmity in the matter. This must be done by someone who saw the thing, and who carries it with anger, and maybe a little bit of hatred in his heart. Is that you Trevor? Go deep now, before you answer me."

Finally, Trevor said, "Yes'm." Just the one word, but it satisfied the woman.

"Good," she said. "Then we've something to discuss."

***

Billy Squier crooned "In The Dark" on Trevor's boom box. Trevor lay on the top bunk, while across the room, Paul pounded a joystick. "Be careful with that thing!" Trevor warned.

Paul said, "It's gonna die soon anyway."

He was right. When the boys opened the gaming console at Christmas, they gazed unbelieving at the box. The machine inside was used, but very real. Nonetheless, one of the joysticks had been broken within a month, its red button jammed down until it wouldn't spring up anymore, and there wasn't any money for repairs. The second stick was held together with duct tape. Both boys knew it wouldn't be with them much longer. Still, they enjoyed it while they could, and Trevor hated to hear Paul abusing the thing. But Paul had always been the nervous one, and Trevor understood that need to expel energy.

For his own part, he reached above his head and turned up the radio. He wanted to get up and pee, but Miss Anna had been clear. Trevor's job was to concentrate his wishes down to the yellow-haired dead man in the bottom bunk, and to not get up for any reason whatsoever until the trouble started. The body had to remember who had killed it, had to remember its own animosity towards its murderer. And it could get that from Trevor, who had watched his stepfather shoot it when it had still been a man. Trevor and Paul had been trapped in their shared bedroom with the blonde corpse for a whole sleepless night now.

"What's that horrible smell?" asked Mom from the doorway.

Paul jumped to his feet, standing so his body blocked

the bed. Paul's job was to keep Mom out of the room when she came home from work. "Where'd you come from?" Paul demanded. "Get outta here! And *knock* first."

Trevor propped himself on one elbow and made a show of looking at their mother. In fact, even that motion was a little difficult right now. Those tendrils of concentration that he had been sending down were also wisps that held him in place and made moving a heavy burden.

"Can't you ask how a lady's night went at work?" Mom said, and then continued without waiting for an answer, "You aren't hiding some other smells, are you?"

"Mom, we're not smoking pot, now let me finish my game! I have to get to the Mothership before time runs out," said Paul.

Mom stood silhouetted in the doorway, leaning on one raised arm. The backlight hid her features, hid the bruises, so that for a moment, her sons saw her as men must have once seen her, a wasp-waisted goddess crying out desire with her very figure. Paul flinched away from the sight, but he stayed between her and the bed.

"I'm just telling you, if that smell isn't gone by the time your Daddy wakes up ..."

"Randy's not our father," Trevor snapped. "Not mine and not Paul's."

"Don't you let him hear you say that," Mom warned. Randy was asleep in his kitchen chair, sprawled backwards in front of an unfinished beer.

"Okay, fine, just let me finish my *game*," Paul insisted.

"I don't know what I'm going to do with you boys.

It's absolutely putrid in that room." But she was retreating down the hall now, and Paul stepped forward to close the door behind her. They knew she was too tired to investigate.

"How are things coming down there?" Trevor asked, his voice sounding as heavy now as his body felt. When the subject wasn't their stepfather, he didn't have much energy for speaking.

Paul approached the bottom bunk and rustled the comforter. "Still dead," he reported to Trevor. "I hope he hurries his yellow head up. Mom's right about the smell, and if Randy wakes up and comes in here …"

"Is she? I guess my nose has kind of adjusted. I hardly notice anymore," Trevor told his brother. "Anyway, it *will* work. Miss Anna said we had to give it a full twelve hours, and we're at eleven and a half right now. And Randy's going to be sleeping awhile yet. I got the pills in his drinks."

Paul nodded, moving away from the bed. Then he picked up his joystick and resumed the task of navigating an alien home to its distant family. "I hope Mom doesn't decide to want the TV back," he said.

"That's a stupid game you're playing if she does" said Trevor. "But she can't come in, and right now, you shouldn't go out.

Paul didn't answer.

"In The Dark" faded out, and the DJ put on some girl band, The Bangles or Bananarama. Trevor groaned and reached behind his head to fiddle with the dial without looking.

Out in the living room, the same song Trevor had just turned down came on louder. Mom keeping herself awake long enough to get some breakfast. Or dinner. It was hard to say which meal was what with a third shift job. Mom sang "She's got it" while Trevor fumbled through stations on a slow-to-tune dial.

"I guess she doesn't want the TV anyway," said Paul.

Mom must have been dodging around Randy's sleeping form, because a couple of times, she stopped singing, then apologized, "Oh! So sorry hon, just getting myself a little dinner, then I'm heading off to bed." And Paul pounded a little harder on the joystick.

Then a bump, and Paul threw down the joystick entirely and spun around to face the bed. Trevor sat up too fast and smacked his head on the ceiling. AC/DC crackled on the boom box, "Back in Black", and Trevor rubbed his skull. The logy feeling let him go as those hundred thousand directed thoughts finally finished their journey through his mind and into the yellow-haired man's body. "Get the blankets off it, Paul," Trevor hissed, as he vaulted down the bunk ladder. The trouble was started.

Paul snatched the cover back, removed the comforter jerkily, then backed against the television. Trevor studied the former man and stood beside his brother.

The corpse's eyes were as yellow as its hair now, and they were glowing. It sat up a little unsteadily, then swiveled its head to look straight at Trevor. "In the kitchen, right?" the dead man rasped.

Trevor nodded, then swallowed hard and spoke.

"Asleep at the table. Not Mom. Not even if she gets in the way."

The corpse nodded, rising until it seemed to fill the small room with its rank smell. "Not Mom," it repeated in that same growling voice. "But when she starts screaming, you be ready to grab her and run. It's going to get ugly when I take that bastard back down with me."

Then, the zombie kicked the door down like it was made of cardboard, while Trevor and Paul huddled together against the TV. "One bright chance," Trevor said. "God almighty, one bright chance."

And then the brothers held on to each other, waiting for their mother to scream.

UPSIDE DOWN
STACEY MESERVY

Blood rushed to my head as I tried to make sense of what just happened. I shook away the cobwebs and realized the truck was upside down.

Instinctively, my hands flew to my belly. I sent up a prayer that the baby would be ok. I still wasn't feeling consistent movement and had no way of knowing if the baby had survived the violent crash.

I moved my head from side to side, trying to figure out if I was hurt and became aware that my blurred vision was because of blood, as was the metallic taste in my mouth. I touched my forehead, but my hand came away clean. I slowly explored my face with my hands, and found the source. A gash ran the length of my chin and was bleeding profusely.

I looked out through the shattered windshield and saw the stars twinkling. It looked so peaceful. The cold winter air seeped into the warm truck and my breath swirled away from me like fog in the early morning. I started to shake, whether from shock, injury or cold, I didn't know.

Seconds felt like hours as I began to feel around for my cell phone. It had been in the cup holder right before the crash. I tried to think of where it might have flown when the truck rolled, but I couldn't see it anywhere. I reached above my head, but all I felt was glass. The smell of smoke hung heavy in the air. I almost called out for help, but the silent night reminded me that until another car traveled this stretch of road, I was on my own.

Panic consumed me, but my reaction was slow. The blood still rushing to my head made me dizzy and the blood seeping out of my chin wasn't helping.

I should have stayed home, I thought.

My crazy pregnant hormones had driven me to make this trip for a sub sandwich and a milkshake. It hadn't seemed dangerous. I knew this stretch of road well but I hadn't even considered black ice.

The truck creaked and I became aware once more that I needed to try to free myself. I reached down and felt for the seat belt buckle. I braced myself for the inevitable fall when it released. I pressed the button but nothing happened. I was still upside down. I pressed it again with more force and again, nothing happened. Pressing frantically, harder and harder, tears welled up in my eyes and panic and fear gripped my heart.

I closed my eyes and took several deep breathes. I wiped the blood away from my eyes again, but this time it was smoke blurring my vision as it rushed in through the shattered windshield. The night was no longer peaceful, and gray smoke covered the stars.

I remembered that my husband always kept a Swiss army knife in the glove box. I thought I could reach it, but was unsure if there was enough time to saw through the seat belt.

As I struggled and strained to reach the glove box, the seatbelt gave way. I was unprepared this time for freedom and landed hard on my side. From my new position, I could see the flames coming from underneath the hood of the truck. I tried the driver side door, but it was stuck. I wriggled over to the passenger side, said a little prayer, and tried the door handle. It budged a little.

I squirmed around and kicked the door with my boot and it creaked open. I climbed through the door and away from the wreckage as fast as I could. When I finally found my footing I stood up and looked behind me to see flames reaching the cabin of the truck. The red paint turned black as night.

If only I had my cell phone, I thought. I stood shivering on the side of the highway watching the truck burn. I felt a sharp pain in my abdomen, then a gush.

It was then that the whole world shifted.

Months later, I sat on the floor of our closet sorting clothes into piles. I had postponed this chore for as long as I could, but it was crunch time. We were moving in two days. Our bedroom looked like we were never leaving.

I divided everything methodically: clothes to donate, clothes to keep, clothes worn beyond donation, clothes to pack in a suitcase until the truck arrived at our new home. Our closet wasn't large, but it seemed to go on forever. I scooted my husband's suit coats over to make sure I had retrieved everything from the shelf.

I drew a sharp breath. One hand flew to my belly as the other covered my mouth. I thought I had boxed everything up, but there, folded neatly on the shelf, was the blanket I had bought for our baby girl. I closed my eyes and was taken back to the night of the accident. I could almost feel the rush of the cold wind on my cheek, the fear when my water broke.

I opened my eyes and stared at the tiny pink blanket. I hesitated, then reached out and picked it up. I closed my eyes again and rubbed the soft material against my cheek. Tears slid silently down my face.

She had been so tiny, with such tiny fingers and a miniature cry. The doctors had given us no reason to hope she would survive. It was quite simply too soon. I could still feel how she fit neatly in the palm of my hands. She had lived for ten minutes. Ten minutes longer than anyone said she would or could. The doctors claimed it was a miracle.

They had someone come in and take pictures, but I had boxed those up too. It was too painful to look at her tiny, perfect form, and to see the two of us huddled around her trying to be a family. The pain in our faces was unmistakable, as unmistakable as the peace on hers when she drew her last breath.

My heart still ached for her. Everyone told me it wasn't my fault, but I couldn't agree. I refused to agree. Guilt seemed to be an adequate punishment. My husband couldn't hide the pain in his eyes and I couldn't help but feel he blamed me too.

If only ... if only I hadn't driven that dark and icy stretch of road, she would still be with us. If only I hadn't been so selfish. If only I had made other choices. There were more "Ifs" than there were hours in a day.

I slumped down on the floor of the closet. The dark cloud that had followed me everywhere for months threatened to overcome me in that moment. The darkness was part of the reason we were moving. I couldn't seem to get away from it, and everyone, my husband included, seemed to think that a change of scenery would help.

I sat there and cradled her blanket and allowed myself to weep for my child, for my loss, for my guilt.

After all the tears were gone, I dried my eyes, carefully folded up the blanket and set it in the box with the rest of my husband's clothes. I knew it was him that had rescued her blanket when I had boxed all of the baby's things.

I was worn out by the emotional effort. It was then that I thought of my little secret. A secret I was afraid to tell anyone just yet. A secret I had only known for a few short days, one that filled me with fear, anxiety and joy all at the same time.

I got up and walked into the bathroom and pulled open my drawer. I dug around till I found the stick and pulled it out to look one more time. Two happy pink lines stared up at me.

I would be so much more careful this time. I would follow all of the guidelines, even if they seemed silly. I had already started to take my prenatal vitamins. I wouldn't let anything or anyone take this blessing away from me again.

I held the pregnancy test for another minute, and then gently returned it to its hiding place.

PICTURE TO PICTURE
RACHEL PADGET

Perched atop the handlebars, she anxiously watches the tread emerging from beneath her. He steers not slowly, but carefully. Still, Clara is glad that she is facing away so that he does not know how closely she is eyeing the wheel, constantly hoping it will not brush her leg, will not snare the bouncing lace of her shoe. A pitch in the road sends her into a momentary sprawl; she recovers with a timorous laugh, which Peter interprets as encouragement. Faster, they roll. Dirt feathers the spokes. She forces her eyes to close and tilts her head in another nervous peal.

Within, worry winds tighter with each rotation of the clanging chain.

Ahead, Don tracks them with his new camera; just before they pass, he hears the satisfying click of time being etched onto film. Next, he waits for Julie, who blows a kiss to the amateur photographer. Allowing his fiancée and his friends to gain a significant lead, Don threads another roll of film into the camera — the third of the day. Julie returns to circle Don as he fumbles with the Kodak's fitted leather case. Energized by the realization that he's about to give chase, Julie dashes past them, toward the bend. Only pieces of her last taunt and the flash of her red bike reach Clara and Peter — the trees scatter her details into a fine confetti. Waving, Peter yells, "Well go on, get her!" His camera safely tucked away, Don also races to fuse with the landscape.

Their friends are a reminder: this road is well travelled. Clara just doesn't know where she and Peter will — *or should* — go, even after all this time. His hand edges closer. Her nerves boil the metal beneath her palms. Rhythmic pedaling ebbs to a slowing coast; the tires find the unworn roadside. She slides off, grateful the only movement is the grass faintly drumming her calves. Tentatively, she smiles at him from safely behind the bike frame. Beside him, ivory petals of a wild tulip glimmer like the gemstone that was not yet meant for her eyes but is meant for her left hand.

Uncertainty grips her.

Then he does.

Her hair and thoughts tangle in his hands. She cannot speak for his lips. His forearms brace her shoulder blades and the back of her knees, lifting her to him. The bike falls. Nothing barricades his kiss.

Disquiet seizes her every muscle until finally, her soles find ground again. He helps to steady her, then puts his hands in her palms with a sigh. "Clara?"

This is the moment, the place, where we will arrive one thing but leave another. Fiancée? Ex? She doesn't want out, but forever is beyond what she is certain she can give. Holding his hands but not his gaze, she notices that her landing has pinched the stem of the flower. "Yeah Peter?"

"Wh — why aren't you kissing me back?"

Carefully circumventing the downed bloom, she toes the ground, wondering if she should also sidestep the question. "I ..." She tethers her gaze to the new dimples in the soil to avoid glancing at the wicker basket where her future may or may not be tucked away. The truth finds its way to her lips anyway, "... I know why you brought us here." Smoothing the ground, she adds, "I found *it*."

He turns away, each fist clutching a shock of hair, "What exactly did you see?"

"The box," she admits, wondering if she assumed too much.

As his oxfords abuse a tree root underfoot, his hands relax and clasp atop his head; sprays of blonde peek from beneath their grip. "And you don't feel the same?"

"I do, but ..."

Fragments of bark flake from the root he abrades, but his frustration is otherwise contained. He gives her ample time to complete her thought, eventually, asking, "You're not a hundred percent sure?"

"Sometimes I am, but questions creep in." She adds tremulously, "Don't they for you?"

Clara thinks she can detect the slightest nod, but Peter shakes off the acquiescence. He finds her waist and rests his cheek against hers; the light press of his jaw helps her decipher his whisper, "What I know is that I'm happy." This time she is the one pursuing a closer touch, edging in until she can just detect the budding whiskers that belie his clean shaven face. The gesture gives him the confidence to form the question he had been reluctant to ask, "Are you?"

"Very." Allowing his embrace to dissolve her distress, the first inklings of love resurface: the goodnight kiss outside her dorm; how, despite wanting him, she managed to fret about the approaching curfew, about who might see. She finally broke away when the monitor rattled her keys. Minutes later, inexplicably, Peter was at Clara's door — *We're going dancing! Yes, NOW. Forget curfew — stay with me until breakfast.* She had willed her eyes to stay open through *Earth Angel* and finally collapsed at daybreak. His fearlessness mystified her, but she loved him. Still glowing in the memory, she repeats, "I'm very happy."

"Then why not?"

Studying the opening in the trees where Julie and Don disappeared, Clara tries, "I guess — It's just ..." She gives up attempting to form an answer. Instead, she asks, "How can you be so sure?"

Two fingers rest against her temple. "Don't do that!" Peter shakes his head and bends to upright the bike. He props it on the tree and opens the basket, "Listen, I know you like to be cautious. To plan. Consider. Know all the facts." Clutching an emerald box, he leans on another tree, "But for once — well, we're never going to know exactly what's down the road for us. That's life!"

Nearby, a wren takes a break from chattering to eavesdrop; in the quiet, Clara can just make out the recurring grate of a tiny box hinge before Peter's voice covers it, "I love you. How can I show you that it's what we *do* know that matters?" This time he leaves the box open, considering what he finds, "You know, I've been carrying this around for two weeks, waiting until it felt right to ask — could've been another year." Snapping the box shut, he returns to the basket, "That was the only question in my mind — not *if*, just when."

Pivoting, Peter assesses Clara, "Actually, that hasn't changed." He tosses the box, catches it, and tilts his hand toward Clara, waiting for permission to reveal the contents within, "It's yours — whether you want it a few minutes or a lifetime of moments."

Her finger is lost in a strip of diamonds and gold.

Breaking tires churn gravel. Startled, Clara and Peter look up — into the lens of Don's camera.

***

The topography of her hands alludes only to the duration of her story — the deep contours and the tributaries of veins that cover her hands will never tell of the children they lifted, the places she signed her name, or the times they rose to cover her cry. Nor do the lines on her face reveal the moments she smiled — only that she did. Her arthritic fingers struggle to remove a photo from its prominent frame. They go down the line, slowly freeing each from its glass encasement. Lost forever on this wall of memories is the life that took place from picture to picture. After 58 years together, he is now gone. In a few months' time, she would be too. Clutching a nearby doorframe, inch by inch, she lowers to her knees. Once there, she pauses, eyeing how distant the friendly help of the door knob seems to be. Gripping a black and white, her shaky but resolute hand seeks out the place where the floor and wall stretch toward each other but fail to join. As she forces the photo into the gap, for a moment, anyway, she feels not pain, but joy. *This way, in some way, we will continue to dwell in our home. Always together.*

    ***

Outside a brick bungalow, a couple poses near a FOR SALE sign; the real estate agent hands them a SOLD banner to cover it, then raises her camera. This photo, which they will hang within the home, will not show everything. The unease he bore about paying the mortgage will be lost to time, as will her uncertainty about the life she would be able to make for the life growing within her. These are ours to carry.

Years later, when they remodel to make room for a third baby, a worker will find a picture of a young couple on a bike, the woman perched atop the handle bars. No one will know that she anxiously watched the tread emerge from beneath her, her worry winding tighter with each rotation of the clanging chain that carried her toward the moment that would set the rest of her life in motion.

HEADING SOUTH, GOING NOWHERE
VICTORIA KIRICHOK

The swirling water going down the drain was purple, not brown as I expected. "Please God," I whispered, "Don't let me go from Marilyn Monroe to Violet Beauregard." When I looked in the mirror I saw that my hair was now a dull brown. I had been check-me-out platinum for a long time, but now it's time to blend in.

Maybe Joey won't follow me. Maybe he'll just move one of his little chippies in for a while. She can play house with him and he'll forget about me. Maybe he'll be so relieved that I didn't clean out the bank accounts that he won't come after me. Maybe.

I put up with his shit for six years and Friday was it — the chippy that broke wifey's back. I demanded to know where he was and what he was doing. I wasn't going to let him buy me off with another trinket. "Who the hell do you think you are?" he asked before he hit me. Joey didn't stick around long enough to hear the answer. He just left me on the floor. The sting on my face smelled like whiskey and cheap women.

I put up with him sleeping around and coming home late. I got used to the nice house and the fancy car and the housekeeper. I liked getting my nails done and working out and shopping. When I saw the back of his hand imprinted on my cheek I realized I was no better than one of his whores. I looked the other way while he screwed strippers so I could live in a big house and drive a nice car.

I traded in all of his shiny tokens of apology for a handful of cash. I left the Lexus at the pawnshop and took a cab to the train station. I paid for a ticket to Chicago with my credit card before I tossed it in a trashcan. Then I walked four miles to the bus station and paid cash for a Grey Hound headed south. I didn't make it easy for him to follow me.

I considered heading to Savannah or New Orleans, figuring it would be easier to blend in. But after sixteen hours on a bus I got off when I saw a cleanish-looking motel near a strip mall. I didn't know if I was in North Carolina or South Carolina, but my ass was numb from the vinyl seats. It was time to take a break, change my look, and plan my next move.

I dried my newly brown hair with the cheap motel hairdryer as best I could and went looking for something to eat. I found a diner a block away from the motel. Bells on the door jingled when I walked in.

"Hey Sweetie," called the waitress behind the counter. "Just sit anywhere."

There were only a handful of people in the place — mostly older folks. Regulars I'd be willing to bet — drinking coffee and chatting. I started toward the counter, but decided on the privacy of a booth.

"You want coffee Honey?" The waitress asked as she handed me a menu.

"Yes, black please." I answered.

"Huh? I thought all you city girls liked those lattes and frappacinos and whatnot."

"Nah. Too fattening." I told her.

"Aw, honey you could use some fattening up." She answered as she poured my coffee. "You look over the menu and let me know when you're ready. My name's Wanda."

"Thanks." I said as I scanned the laminated menu. It was breakfast on one side and lunch on the other. "Are you serving breakfast or lunch right now?"

"Honey, you can get anything you want on that menu any time we're open." She said as she swung her curvy body back to group of regulars in the back to refill their coffee.

I looked the menu over — everything was fried, covered in cheese or came with bacon. Well, maybe putting on a few pounds would help me blend in a little too. It would be a while before I got to another Pilates class.

Wanda returned a few minutes later, "What do you say? Anything on our little menu catch your eye city girl?

You in the mood for breakfast? or will it be lunch today."

"Breakfast." I told her. "I haven't had a big breakfast in way too long."

"Now that's a shame. It's the most important meal of the day."

"So they say. How about this one? The touchdown."

"No messing around for you, eh Sweetie? One touchdown coming up — you want grits or homefries with that?"

"Homefries."

"Coming right up. I'll be back to freshen up your coffee too.

"Thanks Wanda."

I leaned back in my seat, feeling relaxed for the first time since I left. The past few days all I cared about was putting some distance between me and Joey. I needed to know if he was looking for me, but I couldn't think of a single person I could call. When I started dating Joey, all my own friends slipped away.

I always tried to avoid asking questions about what he did for a living. But my real friends, the ones who cared about me asked a lot of questions. I thought they were overreacting and I stopped talking to them. The less I knew the better, as long as I had everything I wanted. He spent way too much money to be a plumber, worked too many hours to be a banker, and wasn't bright enough to be a lawyer. On some level, I always knew he was doing something shady. I just never knew the details.

Wanda put my plate in front of me. There was enough bacon and cheese to require a Surgeon General's warning. But after a day of eating only what I could get at bus stop vending machines, it was fried manna from heaven.

The bells on the diner door jangled and police officer walked in. My heart raced and I reminded myself I had nothing to be afraid of. I was running away, but I wasn't running away from the law.

"'Mornin' Wanda," he said as he removed his hat.

"'Mornin' deputy Stone. The usual?"

"Yes, Ma'am," he said as he sat down at the counter. "I'll have to take it to go this morning though."

I wished I had a book or magazine I could pretend to be reading. I didn't know where to look. I found myself eating faster and faster and staring at my plate.

"Slow down, Honey," Wanda said as she refilled my coffee. You're gonna give yourself a bellyache."

I laughed. For years I had been living on lean protein and salads so I could fit my ass into two hundred dollar jeans. It felt liberating to eat without caring if I gained a few pounds.

"You're right Wanda," I said. "I must've let myself too hungry."

"It's easy to eat too fast here," Deputy Stone said. "The food is almost as good as the service." He winked at Wanda and she playfully swatted him with the menu. I tried to slow down and sip my coffee.

"Are you new in town?" he asked me.

"Yes," I told him as I fiddled with a crust of toast. I hadn't given much thought to a cover story yet. "I'm probably just passing through. I got laid off from my job so I'm looking around for a new place to start."

"What were you doing before?" he asked.

"I was a secretary in a real estate office," I told him, thinking back on the college internship where I met Joey. The truth was, I hadn't been inside an office or a classroom since our first date. He was buying a house and invited me to see it. Joey was cute and charming at first, but it was the house I fell in love with.

I dreamt of preparing meals on those granite countertops, serving Thanksgiving dinner under the dining room's cathedral ceiling, and teaching my children to swim in the sapphire swimming pool. But we only used the granite countertop to eat our take-out salads on, the maid dusted the unused mahogany dining room table once a week, and the children were a wish that never came true — thank God.

Wanda presented Deputy Stone with a white paper bag and a styrofoam coffee cup.

"Well, Miss. I don't know if there's much work to be had here," the deputy said. The corners of his eyes crinkled up when he smiled. "But there aren't many things in life as beautiful as the South in springtime. You picked a mighty nice time to be passing through."

The deputy tipped his hat as he walked out the door. I looked out the window after him as he passed down the street lined with budding magnolia trees. He was right. It was a good time to be passing through.

ABOUT WRITE ON EDGE

Where inspiration meets community.

Write on Edge (formerly The Red Dress Club) was created as a place for writers to gather, exchange ideas and learn something about the art of storytelling.

We welcome any and all writers, regardless of level – anyone interested in writing has a place here. We are also open to writers of all genres: Fiction or non-fiction. Fantasy, young adult, chick lit, memoir – there are no limits.

Even though we have changed our name, we still are inspired by a blog post by Jenny Lawson, The Bloggess, about a Red Dress.

For many of us, our Red Dress is our dream to become a published writer. Maybe we just need a little extra motivation.

Maybe we just have to try to Write on Edge.

Visit us online at **www.writeonedge.com**

ABOUT BANNERWING BOOKS

Bannerwing Books is an independent publishing imprint based in central Massachusetts.

For more information, please visit them online at www.bannerwingbooks.com